Additional Praise for *The Selling Starts When the Customer Says No*

"Our company engaged Bill and Richard to do extensive sales training. Their conference seminars were loaded with superb content and sales techniques. I'm confident that the high marks they earned with us then will certainly transfer to the salesperson who reads their new book."

> —Michael L. Nelson, President and CEO
> *Chrysler Systems Leasing Inc.*

"This is high-quality sales training at its best. *Must* reading for those who choose to lead the pack."

> —John J. Driver, President
> *Ceridian Network Services*

"I'm a young sales professional and I'm determined to be the best that I can be. This no-nonsense, 'how-to' sales book was an investment in my future. I recommend it to anyone who works in the sales trenches and wants to be the best that they can be."

> —Mike J. Wagner, Sales Representative
> *TELEDYNE ALLVAC/VASCO*

THE SELLING STARTS WHEN THE CUSTOMER SAYS NO

THE 12 TOUGHEST SELLS - AND HOW TO OVERCOME THEM

RICHARD S.   O. WILLIAM
SEELYE/MOODY

PROBUS PUBLISHING COMPANY
Chicago, Illinois
Cambridge, England

ISBN 1-55738-446-0

Printed in the United States of America

BB

1 2 3 4 5 6 7 8 9 0

JB/BJS

DEDICATION

TO OUR CUSTOMERS, OUR FRIENDS WHO SELL, COM-
PETITORS WHO CAVED IN, FAMILIES WHO WERE RELENT-
LESS, AND TO OUR EGO AND GREED; THEY ALL HELPED.

Thanks also to the works of Alan S. Schoonmaker. They
added insight about sales processes and personality traits.
Our special appreciation for the editing skills of Carol Y. Ost.
She was our secret weapon!

TABLE OF CONTENTS

CHAPTER 12
IMPLEMENTING CHANGE IN YOUR ACCOUNTS   233

Tough Sell: Putting on a New Face with Old
Customers

*Taking what you have and
making it better than ever*

PREFACE

In sales, some people are always more successful than others. There are reasons why this is so and many of them are constant, no matter what kind of selling you do. However, each category (i.e., retail, wholesale, business-to-business, and so on) of selling also has unique characteristics that must be mastered and applied consistently to achieve the status of a top performer.

Parts of this book will help any salesperson to improve his or her skills; however, the book is intended for those who sell business-to-business. We have written for the seasoned "pro" who wants to recapture forgotten skills and for the new salesperson who wants to augment enthusiasm with successful selling strategies, techniques and sales skills.

In business-to-business selling, the salesperson is given a roadmap showing how to get the job done. The product or service is well defined; territory responsibilities, sales quotas, incentive plans and so on are all succinctly spelled out by the company. You know the road you're supposed to travel, but soon discover that it is loaded with hazards where accidents always seem to happen. These accidents are the tough selling situations that slow you down or even cause your selling efforts to crash!

We are not talking about customer objections, which we view as normal selling impediments that should be quickly dispatched by most salespeople. This book talks about major obstacles that you didn't plan for or that you knew little about. The character of tough selling situations is such that the only real defense is to preempt or defuse them before they escalate—a defense called *account development*. That is the theme of this book. Account development is a salesperson's guide for integrating objectives into account selling opportunities. It is an aggressive, proactive process that anticipates probable events and formulates strategies to overcome the downside potentials. The account development process becomes a roadmap of activities and skills necessary to achieve sales strategies.

This book is a "hands-on" sales tool designed to help you combat and win the day-to-day difficulties found in real sales situations. It will motivate you to higher levels of professional selling by sharing new insights, reviving and polishing sales skills and showing how to start making things happen *your* way.

Our views and techniques are validated by years of selling and hundreds of experiences. The conclusions and solutions are not academic or hypothetical. They are smart, no-nonsense ways to deal successfully with the tough world of selling. There are tremendous rewards for becoming as good as you're capable of becoming!

So take our book home today . . . and start using it tomorrow! And the next time your customer says, "No, I don't think so, because . . .," you'll know what to do—and just how to do it!

CHAPTER 1

MENTAL TOUGHNESS

A Tough Selling Situation:

When Distractions and Anxieties
Cause You to Lose Focus

When you can't keep your mind in one place, you can't be effective in any place. Every selling situation becomes tough because your concentration is gone and your attention span is so short. Unresolved personal situations mount one upon another and slowly each drains your energy. You sense your loss of direction but are unable to chart a new course.

————

BRUCE

The dash clock said 7:20 P.M. when Bruce suddenly realized that he had been just sitting in his car for almost half an hour. He couldn't retrace where his mind had been for the past thirty minutes. A tear slowly moved down his cheek, and he rubbed it away to the whispered accompaniment of several four letter words. Kathy would have picked up their daughter, Sarah, and been home by six. She'd be wondering where he was. Bruce dug for his key, knowing he wouldn't get there before eight o'clock. She wasn't going to be a happy camper, but she hadn't been happy for months. Kathy's Mom had offered to keep Sarah—how many times? Bruce didn't want that. Ever since Kathy's parents sprang for the honeymoon trip, it was like they had also bought a license to butt in.

Bruce pulled away from the office parking lot and knew that the drive home was a good time to analyze the day's sales activities. His mind danced quickly through several sales call situations but didn't linger on any particular event. None of them seemed important and tomorrow would probably be the same.

Kathy hated putting Sarah in day-care, and now she comes up with weekly reasons why she hates her job. Every night it's either a day-care problem or a job problem. Well she's just going to have to tough it out 'cause we need her paycheck—not to get ahead, just to stay even.

Bruce hit the ramp onto 95, accelerated into the flow of traffic, moved over to the fast lane, and forgot to turn the radio on. He didn't know why he had shouted at Betty Thompson today. Gee, she was just trying to do her job. He wished he had apologized. Even so, she could have been more careful. She just sat there and didn't say a word. Bruce thought that Betty was too old to still be working anyway.

He could admit that he wasn't making as many customer calls as he should. There were too many other things to think about. Bruce felt guilty about slipping away yesterday to catch an afternoon movie. He had gotten lost in someone else's troubles for about two hours. It had seemed like a diversion that he needed. He could have spent that time with a loyal customer but he hadn't arranged to do that.

Through the soft fog his headlights picked up the first Stamford exit sign. He wished his in-laws lived in Arizona instead of Greenwich. Bruce was trying to be analytical, but his mind wouldn't stay focused in one place long enough to select a subject to analyze. To hell with it anyway.

Selling can be very rewarding, both in terms of dollars and of personal satisfaction resulting from doing a job well. Still, it is a hard business. An important sales call or selling presentation requires a clear mind and intense concentration. Customer responses must be immediately understood or clarified with proper questioning techniques. A salesperson must be alert to opportunities to insert the benefits of his or her products and services with a smooth and logical flow. The presentation must be convincing and also show a problem solving attitude that captures the interest and involvement of the prospect. In short, they need to be at the top of their game!

Lots of bad stuff can happen when you're in a consequential selling situation and you aren't attentive to and entirely focused on that situation. The most important consequence is that your call will be poorly executed and therefore you'll seldom achieve your objectives. If your *condition* continues, selling performance will diminish until you become completely dejected. Salespeople must recognize that dealing successfully with personal distractions and resulting anxieties are prerequisites to effective selling. We all need to understand techniques that can help in the recognition, the cure, and future prevention of such situations.

Mental toughness is a conceptual extension of mental health. Its adaptation is partially promoted by the knowledge that others will intrude into your space, bringing situations and problems that can cause you to become involved and distracted. If left unattended, many distractions have the potential to cause anxiety. Confronting distractions, even as they are taking shape, is much better than allowing them to grow and take on added dimensions. This mental toughness alludes to recognizing an event or situation that is becoming a distraction, and beginning an automatic process of dealing with it. Perhaps the essence of mental toughness is that when a problem is recognized, it should be dealt with immediately—not later. Attacking such problems can be distasteful and can even lead to further conflict. However, it is the best course of action.

Facing your distraction simply means taking actions designed to neutralize it or change it into something less complex and less mind-consuming. Initially, it is an analysis and organization of a situation based on its characteristics. This action opens the way for understanding how volatile the situation is, what can be done now, and who should be doing it. The next step is to attach and assign one or more action items to the situation. *Someone (you or another person) should do something.* When this process is successful, the distraction is converted into a situation undergoing change. Therefore, it should not require your attention again until the change is complete. It follows then that the distracting situation can be mentally filed away for now and retrieved only when (and if) new actions become necessary. Anxieties are far less likely to be associated with situations that you know are undergoing constructive change. The process positions you to bounce away from the consuming aspects of lingering distractions and move quickly toward productive activities. You will be displaying characteristics of resiliency and this resilience should be your goal.

Resiliency is the most important objective of our discussion on mental toughness. In these pages we talk about damage control techniques that we believe can help many people learn how to bounce back quickly (or bounce away) from common distracting situations. Strength and inner satisfaction that result from confronting personal distractions, help you to build *and to practice* a resilient attitude. When complete, the resilient attitude is self-energizing and through frequent use, becomes like a good habit. Though you will continue to initially feel the sting caused by outside distractions, you will have a much better chance of staying on your feet. Your resilient attitude *habit* is always ready!

The resilient attitude is not a mind game. Once you solve a problem situation, the conscious process supplies you with a specific experience, or model that you can use again and again to solve similar problems. You don't have to reinvent the wheel because these models are real and all are firmly fixed within your resilient attitude. You now have the security of knowing that new problem situations are solvable by the process. Therefore, lingering distractions are defeated by contained emotions, applied logic, and your resilient attitude. This inner security is your generic road map leading toward a focused "can-do, will-do" state of mind. The supporting platform for this condition is made of reality recognition, determination, integrity and self-control. Positive resiliency is the result.

SOURCES OF DISTRACTIONS

Many people will intrude into your space, bringing situations and problems to your attention. Fortunately, most of these do not distract you because there is no expectation or reason for you to take part ownership of the situation. In such cases, it is merely shared information. You may discuss the situation and even offer advice, ending with something like "I really hope that it will work out okay."

However, your family environment offers the potential for significant distractions. It is here that joint ownership and expectations become common characteristics of most situations. It is easy to understand how they quickly become distracting. While we cannot give you a plan to prevent family generated distractions, we will present some strategies for dealing with them.

Family Distractions

Family relationships can bring the greatest joy and the greatest moments of disappointment. Those joyous times can make you feel like you're walking on clouds and help you stay near the top of your game. These relationships are bonded with love, caring, and blood. As you would expect, situations that evolve out of these relationships often go far beyond causing distractions—they have high impact and can quickly lead to anxiety! Your goal is to resolve these situations so that you gain some acceptable level of "peace of mind" and can then go about your business without constant distraction.

In this regard, there is an approach that seems to foster success. It has only three dimensions. However, these are beyond the capabilities of many people and most of us have some limitations upon our level of achievement. They are: understanding the bonds, understanding and accepting reality, and acceptance of oneself and tolerance of others.

Depending on the circumstances, you may be dealing with confused siblings, hungry creditors, a vindictive spouse, splintered assets, harassment, attorneys, and all the other fallout junk. Each of these will qualify as a principal distraction. However, the trick is to accept that you're not trying to fix them so much as you're just trying to work your way through them. Distractions being worked on are not as injurious as known distractions laying dormant.

Here is a simple analogy: Many of us start and maintain a list called "Things to Do." When an item is transferred from an abstract problem to the list, it usually becomes less annoying. Once on the list, it will appear to be in process, and is therefore under control. Similarly, it is better to work toward changing the characteristics of a distracting problem than to allow them to solidify. The change means that you are taking action. You are replacing a distraction with action and new events. Your actions now supersede the original distraction and the possibility of anxiety is deferred.

Your ability to deal with the family problems is greatly enhanced when you can:

- Know that you don't have to be perfect;
- See the new situation with clarity;
- Get it identified as an issue;
- Address it quickly;
- Get a plan in place;
- Work through it candidly;
- Resolve it, dispatch it, shelve it;
- Move on to other things.

And finally, the family situations go much smoother when you have addressed other facets of your environment that spawn distractive situations. We need to look at some examples of these.

Acceptance of Oneself

You are not a perfect person. There's lots of room for improvement. The good news is that you probably aren't so bad after all. You're tolerable and others have found much in you to admire and care about. We know that it's written somewhere that just being "you" is okay, and we promote that conclusion. We want you to buy into this conclusion . . . otherwise you can't go forward.

Understanding Your Values and Beliefs

It is worthwhile to take time out and consciously think about who you are and then get very firm with the conclusions. The objective here is to be uncompromising in the things that you are, as well as the things you are not. For example, suppose you say that you are honest. You want to always be honest and are willing to make that a basic value. If you compromise it in any way, you're going to undermine your mental toughness.

Some examples of other values or beliefs will help to relate to our focus here. You may also interchange the words "value/belief" with *"some things that are important to me."*

Generosity: I like to make people feel good.

Independence: I've reached maturity. I don't need to consult to reach my conclusions. I will not accept undue influence and even less control.

Tolerance: I'm willing to accept the way most people are and how they think. I want the same for me and can sometimes insist on it.

Beliefs: Experience, logic, and reasoning have conditioned me to think certain things and therefore to act certain ways. I'm comfortable with these beliefs. They have become my mental friends. Over time, some get modified, others begin to form and sometimes, one gets tossed out. I trust my beliefs, and I will try hard to respect the beliefs of others.

These are only a small subset of the kinds of values that are gathered together for any one of us. To a large part, they are who we are and why we are all so different. We suggest sewing all these values/beliefs into your resilient attitude because they give constant strength and direction.

Pride as a Strong Resource

There is another stabilizing element woven into the fabric of "who you are." The word "stabilizing" is carefully selected because we think that this element is much like an onboard gyroscope, in that it will add balance to the things that you do . . . and the things that you will allow to be done to you. We are talking about your pride.

There are at least two kinds of pride, and seldom does one person have both kinds. We believe that only one is an asset and adds anything to one's mental toughness. This is the kind of pride that is chain-linked to your self-esteem and to your self-respect. In this regard it is truly part of the system that helps you to navigate through tough situations and their frustrating distractions. *It is a quiet and deeply ingrained strength and is self-validating.* It causes you to do good and admirable acts and to behave in predictable ways. You cannot allow it to be invaded or seriously compromised.

The other kind of pride is vanity (false pride). Some people carry this about on their shoulders and it becomes a visible part of their outward personality. It shouts out their haughtiness and leads to routine arrogance. It is a protective facade that shields flawed values and beliefs. This flavor of pride is a weakness and has nothing to offer our mental toughness concept.

The Money Distraction

Any part of your environment where demand always exceeds supply can easily become a root source for testy situations. *Affection and time* have these characteristics but few things cause distracting problems as quickly or as frequently as MONEY.

You make money and you use money. You work for money, mainly to satisfy needs that you have. You also have wants, and if you have enough money, you can allocate some to your wants. We don't think that having too much money is going to be your problem, so we won't deal with that aspect. Problems are most likely generated by not having enough money for your needs and wants. Therefore, how you use what you have, gets to the "issue" category very quickly.

If you share the money that you have (that you earn) with someone else, the "use" issue becomes expanded. For the purposes of our discussion, let's assume that the sharing is done with spouse and/or spouse and children. If you've established "use of money" ground rules for yourself, then it follows that you have the right to (and should) extend your rules, or establish special ones, for those who share the use of your money.

Those who use money earned by someone else may not place the same values on its use as did the provider. That is to say that they may want, or choose, to use it differently. The sharee and the sharer will come to different conclusions.

We know that shared money can be a source of problems and real distractions. To minimize or avoid these requires that the money earner follow a pattern that shows the importance of money, its conservation, and how to use it. "What is mine is also yours" won't work unless the sharee and sharer are completely in sync on the use of money. It is not automatic nor does it just happen because of caring and love. So think about use of money in terms of avoiding money dilemmas and the resulting distractions.

Admit That You Need a Solution

The nature of your environment is such that a continuous bombardment of problems that can distract you is pretty much inevitable. The question is "How full is your plate when the new one comes along?" If it's overflowing, you were already in big trouble to the extent that you can't deal with the new one. You're much too busy perpetually doing a lousy job with the old garbage to be very effective dealing with the new stuff.

This of course, isn't where you want to be. You can't work your way out of it quickly. You are definitely off your game and are being distracted in more ways than you know. Yes, we know that in a moment of frustration you can say that you just aren't going to deal with these things today. What you say doesn't matter much and has very little to do with the effect this heap of little problems is having on your ability to perform. This troublesome little pile affects more than just job performance; it affects performance in most areas of your day-to-day activities. There are ways to resolve these problems.

The Resolution Process

There is a technique that many people already use. They could use it better and more frequently if they became more conscious about the mechanism. The first step is to identify the problem or situation. At this point, your problem can likely be broken into smaller pieces. These pieces should be assessed and analyzed. After this analysis, the problem usually isn't nearly as bad as was first contemplated. Thus, the original situation or problem has been downsized and now may look very different and not nearly as complex. It may look more like an inconvenience that is trying to act like a distracting problem. To the extent this process has been successful, we're now better able to deal with it.

Deal with distractions as they become identified. Never let them mount up, one upon the other. To do this, you'll need a modus operandi that can automatically jump-start. You'll need a practiced formula so that you don't have to reinvent. This means that you have already resolved an approach that you use for the major categories that seem to spin off the most problems and/or distractions. Not only have you identified and practiced the approach, but you've used it to resolve how you feel and how you deal with numerous key issues.

As a result, you've galvanized an attitude. This attitude has become real; it exists and you have it with you every day. You know that you have analyzed major categories, taken certain actions that have allowed you to "think" of them as "finished" and put them safely away on a mental shelf. Notice that we didn't say that they were finished, but only that you firmly think of them as finished for the moment. These problem-solving techniques should then become standard operating procedure for you because you will have carefully constructed and believe in each. The reality of this attitude helps you to step confidently into each new day.

And finally, we never thought that if you could weave the fabric of mental toughness, you'd be free of distractions. But we did want to share a way that we do believe can help many readers as they go about the process of moving from one day to another.

Initially, we said that selling is a hard job. If you sell, you know how important it is to be attentive and completely focused on the selling situation at hand. If distractions have matured into anxieties, then you won't sell as well as you're capable of selling. Your model of mental toughness can become your special way of avoiding the trap.

BRUCE'S SOLUTION

Over the next few days, Bruce realized how overwhelmed he was by all the distractions that seemed to grow and accompany him from one day to the next. He concluded that his job was not the source of his problems but that both he and his job were becoming victims. He decided it was time to take action to resolve these problems. He found that he needed to assess the problems and assign ownership of them. Since Kathy was part of his support system, he asked her to participate in the resolution process.

Bruce and Kathy decided to break down the big problem into smaller, more manageable parts. Bruce decided that he had somehow assumed ownership of Kathy's unhappiness in her job and realized that this was not something in his control. Kathy agreed that she needed to own the problem and work out her own resolution.

They decided to share the ownership of the problems with day-care and both agreed that this was a real reason that caused Kathy to feel discontent with her job. Kathy thought that she might feel better about leaving Sarah if her mother played a more active role in day-care. Bruce realized that his pride in this instance was counterproductive and was preventing him from seeking help from his mother-in-law to take care of Sarah.

Their financial problems might take longer to resolve, and Bruce and Kathy decided they would share the responsibility for working them out. They would evaluate their spending and find out if changes could or needed to be made. The key was to be flexible in any solution they devised.

Bruce felt better already. He and Kathy had successfully identified the problems, assigned ownership, worked out an action plan, and were ready to press on. He was confident he had the mental toughness to focus on his selling at work; *and tomorrow he would apologize to Betty.*

As Bruce and Kathy began to focus on activities and solutions, their attitudes improved and the attention conflict between family and job became easier to deal with. They were unconsciously building new models that would be available to them in similar situations. *They learned that problems being dealt with were not nearly so distracting as problems laying dormant.*

We think that Bruce and Kathy have laid a foundation that can start their journey toward building mental toughness *together.* As they continue openness and honesty with each other, their resiliency in the face of new distractions and anxieties will be quicker and more certain.

So what happened to Bruce and his job as a professional salesman? Did he develop the skills necessary to identify and cope with personal distractions? Will he sneak away to afternoon movies and then rationalize the escape? Will his mind be freed to concentrate on the tough job of business-to-business selling? Will he incorporate selling strategies and techniques found in this book?

The story could have many endings. However, Bruce has successfully passed the *first and most difficult of all the tough selling situations!* Therefore, we are going to color his future bright and golden.

CHAPTER 2

ACCOUNT DEVELOPMENT

A Tough Selling Situation:

Dealing with the Unexpected

This tough selling situation happens to all of us at one time or another. Buyers are not obligated to tell us about changes or new developments in their company. If you have only a few contacts in your account, they may not even know of impending changes. You cannot rely on the past for a picture of the future.

ROBERT

Robert's mind played with the rejection his whole body seemed to feel. Last Friday morning he had been told that the annual buy agreement from National Industrial Aids hadn't been renewed. Moreover, it wasn't going to be renewed. Robert had no idea that National had transferred responsibility for the design and acquisition of internal forms to their Dallas facility. He'd had this business sewed up for the past three years. National's monthly orders were automatic, happening like clockwork, with last year's totaling slightly over $100,000. It was something Robert had planned on; National's purchase numbers had even been built into his quota objectives.

His local buyer contact hadn't known, until he tried to process Robert's routine bid, that the contract would be issued by the Dallas people. The buyer, Scott Harding, was also surprised that the requirements had not been passed through his office as usual. Scott gave Robert his Dallas counterpart's name, but that guy took three days to answer Robert's phone calls; and when he did, he told Robert that National had already let a contract to Key Design LTD out of Montreal. Robert had never even heard of Key Design!

Robert's mind whirled with the trouble this was going to cause. Should he go to Dallas? What should he tell his boss? National was almost 10 percent of Robert's revenue. How was he going to replace it? He quickly calculated that this was going to be a $6,000 hit on his own income. He needed to understand what had gone wrong, and he needed a recovery plan. Robert fanned through the pages of his control book. Repeat business, like National's, may represent as much as 80 percent of the year's revenue, he thought. I've got to get National back.

If you are a busy salesperson, you will likely encounter one or more of the following tough challenges at least weekly:

- Resistance to change

- Entrenched competition
- A prospect who won't see you
- A negative perception or lack of perception of your product or company
- Tons of effort with no results
- New product introduction
- Imposed constraints by your company
- Too much to do; inability to do a thorough job
- Indecisive customers
- Irate customers

Timing can be everything; knowing when these situations are going to occur would be helpful, but is unlikely. However, if you have a good Account Development program in place, you will have some control over the conditions that surround a new and testy situation.

Account Development is positioning yourself in your customer's environment so you can gather information that will allow you to realize (harvest) the potential business that can come your way. Through Account Development you can establish multiple, good contacts, at many levels within the customer organization.

Account Development is like an Individual Retirement Account (IRA) because you're investing in and protecting your future. It is also somewhat different from an IRA because you can take dividends without paying an early withdrawal penalty. Account Development also has mutual fund characteristics in that your time and efforts toward Account Development investments are diversified and can be made in modest but steady amounts. Again, like the mutual fund, suddenly one day you realize that your investments have accumulated more value than you'd thought. These investments are metered in the time you spend with customer personnel who don't buy anything, except maybe other companies or perhaps consulting services. However, as sales-people, selling to someone who doesn't buy goes against all of our killer instincts. We want action NOW!

The question that begs for an answer is if the customers don't buy anything, what do you sell them? Well, they do buy *into* things, but they don't buy exactly what you are employed to sell. They buy into ideas and into solution frag-ments if these lean toward problems or opportunities that are of some interest to them. They might buy into a unique course of action taken by one of your other customers. They might have an interest in a new technology, even if it is somewhat remote from their immediate projects. They might listen to encounters your company is experiencing in a foreign market.

Somewhere in all of this is a business relationship that can surface and grow, providing a link to a contribution you and your company can make. It is your job to cultivate it. Your hidden agenda is to position yourself and your product on the inside track. When successfully executed, this means that you've done lots of selling!

Most business buyers buy what they are told to buy. The people you want to get next to are the "tellers." There are lots of tellers, and they are usually telling each other before they tell the buyers. Account Development is your way of interfacing with the tellers. Then when they get around to telling the buyers, they are likely to incorporate some of your ideas into the buying parameters. Isn't that what you always wanted?

As "buy time" approaches, you will be working with those who buy or advise the buyer. They will quickly figure out that you know more about the application of the products to be purchased than most of your competitors do. They'll also recognize that you have an insider's understanding of what happened to cause the need as reflected by their pending purchase. You probably could enlighten them about the logic behind some of the specifications received in their di-rection from above. You are positioned to help them avoid making mistakes and/or just wasting time by looking at the wrong product solutions. A thorough Account Development job can result in all of the above and more!

THE TWO PARTS OF THE SELLING CYCLE: VISIBLE AND INVISIBLE

As proficient salespeople, we recognize that a sale has a beginning and an end, and that a sale almost never happens in a single day. We accept the idea of a "selling cycle" and have developed techniques designed to help sniff out the order status and move things in our direction. The targets for Account Development are generally defined as those people and influences not readily visible or obvious, which have had, or may have, or can be motivated to have, an impact upon the characteristics of a selling cycle.

Think of a selling cycle as having two parts: A and B. Part A is *invisible* to many salespeople because it involves higher-level management (the targets) who function behind the scenes. The major decisions are made during the invisible part of the cycle. These decisions later produce the characteristics found during part B of the cycle, the *visible* part.

For example, a decision to increase production capacity would be made by management types who reside on the invisible part of the selling cycle. The visible part of the selling cycle involves buyers, users, and well-defined product requirements. The decision to increase production capacity, for example, will eventually be translated into many requirements such as new machine tools, additional space and more plant workers. The activities needed to obtain these resources are handled by people who function in the visible part of the selling cycle.

These targets (management types) will cause one or more selling cycles to happen. (They can also cause a coup de grâce at any time.) They are the driving forces who begin to formulate solutions as they go about the process of addressing business problems. Their ideas and decisions are passed down within the management structure. During this downward movement, resources needed to carry out the solutions are identified, and plans to gather or acquire these resources begin to appear.

These events cause selling cycles to become visible. We use "cycles" here because the solutions may generate needs that can only be satisfied by many products and services. In such cases, the buying processes can potentially span a wide array of purchase requirements. The visible part of the selling cycle is left in the hands of lower-level (but trusted) managers who become the buyers or direct advisors to the buyer. With direction from above (the targets), they will develop precise specifications to select vendor candidates, to request proposals and arrange for vendor presentations, and, if applicable, to see demonstrations.

However, and more importantly, keep in mind that the invisible part of a selling cycle always precede the visible part. The invisible part of the cycle is given birth by business strategy sessions held months earlier. Everything streams from those sessions, and associated activities begin to fall out and flourish week by week. (See Table 2.1.)

IDENTIFYING YOUR TARGETS

It is plausible to assume that at some time, and at some level, organizations are focusing on particular business situations along with their potential opportunities and problems. During these times a salesperson with a good Account Development program in place would have an excellent chance of "intercepting" opportunity at invisible parts of the selling cycle. To do this, you must know the players and understand their focus. Table 2.2, Intercept Targets, can help in a general way to label these targets and to caption what their focus is likely to be. You'll notice that the "players" are listed on the chart by descending titles. The board of directors is distant from any "buyers" within the organization because their focus is long range. Months may pass before a

Figure 2.1—Business Systems

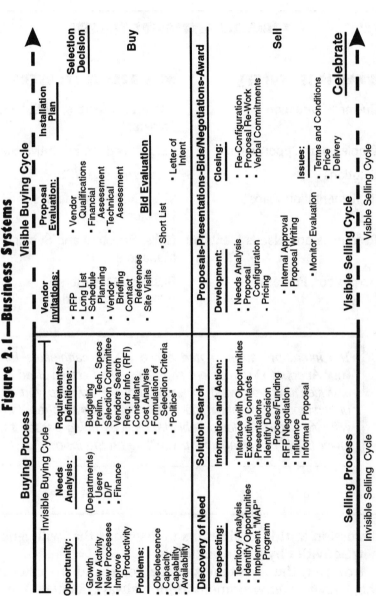

Buying Process

Visible Buying Cycle

Selection Decision

Buy

Installation Plan

Proposal Evaluation:
- Vendor Qualifications
- Financial Assessment
- Technical Assessment

Bid Evaluation
- Short List
- Letter of Intent

Vendor Invitations:
- RFP
- Long List
- Schedule Planning
- Vendor Briefing
- Contact References
- Site Visits

— Invisible Buying Cycle —

Requirements/ Definitions:
- Budgeting
- Prelim. Tech. Specs
- Selection Committee
- Vendors Search
- Req. for Info. (RFI)
- Consultants
- Cost Analysis
- Formulation of Selection Criteria
- "Politics"

Needs Analysis:
(Departments)
- Users
- D/P
- Finance

Opportunity:
- Growth
- New Activity
- New Processes
- Improve Productivity

Problems:
- Obsolescence
- Capacity
- Capability
- Availability

Selling Process

Visible Selling Cycle

Sell

Celebrate

Proposals-Presentations-Bids/Negotiations-Award

Closing:
- Re-Configuration
- Proposal Re-Work
- Verbal Commitments

Issues:
- Terms and Conditions
- Price
- Delivery

Development:
- Needs Analysis
- Proposal Configuration
- Pricing
- Internal Approval
- Proposal Writing
- Monitor Evaluation

Invisible Selling Cycle

Solution Search

Discovery of Need

Information and Action:
- Interface with Opportunities
- Executive Contacts
- Presentations
- Identify Decision Process/Funding
- RFP Negotiation
- Influence
- Informal Proposal

Prospecting:
- Territory Analysis
- Identify Opportunities
- Implement "MAP" Program

TABLE 2.2—INTERCEPT TARGETS

WHAT IT IS (FOCUS)	WHO DOES IT (PLAYERS)
Business Direction	Board of Directors, CEO, President
Problems or Opportunities	CEO, President, Executive Staff
Solutions	Presidents and VP's
Implementation Plans	VP's, General Managers, Directors
Resources and Needs Identified	GM's, Directors and Senior Managers
Acquisition Process	Business Managers, Administrators and Staff

> *The Intercept Targets noted above are all candidates for your Account Development strategies. They are involved in activities that you want to know about. They help you to understand the potential that this account has to offer. You will also know the logic behind directions being passed to lower levels of management. You'll be on the inside.*

---

discussion at this level results in decisions that will generate new activities by the lower levels.

However, the remoteness of the board and the CEO from the "buying" environment is not always factual. We can recall several situations in smaller companies where the board reserved final approval for purchases that exceeded a specified dollar amount. Acquisition specifications, competitive evaluations, and vendor selection did happen at lower levels in these instances, but everything was kicked back upstairs for final reviews and conclusions. We could not assume, in these situations, that the board gave rubber stamp approvals. The board can approve, delay, and even ask that alternatives be explored. Their actions can open the whole process again. An effective Account Development program will anticipate these possibilities and execute activities designed to minimize the downside.

Understanding what is happening (and who is doing it) in the invisible part of the process is essential to even beginning to plan an Account Development effort for any account. Table 2.3, Invisible Part of Sell Cycles, offers more insight into "their considerations" and "their conclusions," which could have a major future impact on the whole company. Notice that in the fifth month, company management concluded that an acquisition represents an option that could move their previously stated business direction ahead at a greatly accelerated pace. Such a solution will excite activity at multiple levels and will move both horizontally and vertically within the organization. It is likely that a high-level group will be formed to explore the possibility of acquiring "Life Care Systems." It can be assumed that there are reasons why (information) the board feels that Life Care Systems is a viable acquisition candidate.

To speed up the process, it is likely that, concurrently with the acquisition process, direction is passed to subordinate levels to study the implementation and integration of a new "what if" acquisition. At this point, the specific acquisition target is probably being described as a hypothetical situation. Even so, it will start to generate implementation plans, which will then lead to the documentation of needs. Nothing may happen, or, more likely, an unexpected press release will suddenly announce the acquisition of Life Care Systems. Again, the beginnings of the visible sales cycle are taking shape. Think about the chart and marvel at the many implications!

TABLE 2.3—INVISIBLE PART OF SELLING CYCLES

THEIR CONSIDERATIONS	THEIR CONCLUSIONS
Business Direction (Month 1-2)	We should expand our offerings in this industry.
Opportunities (Month 3-4)	Special programs for senior citizens would position us into a major growth segment.
Solution (Month 5-6)	An acquisition such as Life Care Systems would be our quickest route.
Implementation Plans (Month 6-8)	We could integrate all administration into our Boston offices.
Needs Identification (Month 9-10)	We'll need more space, equipment, and expanded networks.
Acquisition Process (Month 11-12)	Let's get our purchasing people involved so they'll know where we're going.

Consequential decisions are made in the invisible part of the selling cycle. Steps beyond those outlined above are only in response to what has gone before. Generally, 90 percent of Account Development takes place within the boundaries of the invisible part. The higher you can climb toward month "one," the more effective you will become.

INTERCEPTING TARGETS

An interesting and very practical way to think about Account Development is as if it were an intercept mission. The salesperson starts the mission based on an informed assumption that within the account organization, plans and activities are underway and that, at some point, some of them may point toward the need for the products or services you sell. Your mission is to identify where the plans and activities are located and to gain intelligence about them early on. At its lowest performance level, this part of the mission could be classified as focused snooping. At the high end of the scale, this activity will take the form of carefully selected and executed calls on the account's key managers.

One important difference between these two intercept methods, assuming each produced identical information, is that the snooped data is difficult to validate. Additionally, the fact that it surfaced was highly dependent on the luck of your timing.

Information gathered by roaming the halls is called "public data." This means that the event has already occurred or is about to occur. An intercept at this point is probably in the visible part of the selling cycle, which means that all specifications are in place and the "war" has been declared. Information gathered in a "key management" call may also be almost public data but might refer to an in-process (unfinished) plan. An intercept at this point has the potential to lock onto target before bombs are away!

IMPLEMENTING ACCOUNT DEVELOPMENT

Account Development is a selling process designed to increase the opportunity for and the odds of obtaining new business within a particular customer or prospect account. In order to define your specific selling strategies, you need to take the following steps:

1. *Gather information from the account:* Who uses products like yours? What specific applications include the use of products like yours? Are they expanding or cutting back? Who is writing the *needs* specifications and where do they get their direction from?

2. *Assimilate this information:* What does it all mean? Are there patterns that can help you define where your effort should be concentrated?

3. *Extrapolate business opportunities:* How good are your chances in this account? Will the potential payoff be worth the investment of an Account Development effort?

4. *Feed service benefits back into the account:* How receptive are customer contacts? Did you see areas where your value-added benefits could make a difference to this customer? Do they understand your company's commitment to quality and service?

Implied in the process is the recognition that different kinds of information exist with different customer employees who function in various capacities and levels within the organization. Therefore, the Account Development process and its implementation continue to broaden the customer contact base via both horizontal and vertical call activity. Over time, this leads to increased acceptance of you, the salesperson, as well as of your company and your product or services. You will learn to use this status in such a way that at "buy time" you'll have much more control over your destiny. The degree to which this can happen depends on many things, but foremost among them is how you accomplished item #4 above. This is where you can have a role in *shaping* some of the criteria that the buyers will have as their directions from above. Remember, this shaping is done in the *invisible* part of the selling cycle.

ROBERT'S SOLUTION

An unexpected event is always potentially a tough selling situation simply because the event was a surprise. If the event was only in the planning stage, there might be opportunities for actions that could change it or even prevent it from happening. Such opportunities could exist only if Robert had gathered the information necessary to lead him toward understanding his situation and deducing the possible outcomes. However, Robert was not positioned to gather such intelligence from National Industrial Aids and therefore could not set up any selling strategies. Perhaps Robert could not have learned everything about what was going on, but he could have sniffed out enough to take some evasive actions.

It appears that National's business was a significant part of Robert's revenue stream, and yet he thought of it—and treated it—as though it were automatic and his due! He was not in touch with changes occurring in his account, and these changes came together to cause an event that hurt him. Salespeople must accept the reality that within any business, job functions and responsibilities are constantly shifting.

How you react to an unexpected event depends on the finality of the event. When you can recognize the elements before they take final form, you may have an opportunity to reshape the characteristics of an impending event. But Robert didn't see the elements! When an event has already happened, and is cast in concrete, there is seldom a reaction that can reverse it. Therefore, the only viable technique to overcome this situation is to *prevent* it from happening.

Robert can overcome the potential for future lost business by introducing Account Development into all of his accounts. This is the best way to retain and grow his customers' business. Gathering information, analyzing the data, determining new business opportunities, and positioning himself and his company's products and services as the solution to his customer's problems will give him the advantage over his competition when it's time to close the sale.

CHAPTER 3

BUSINESS MANAGEMENT STRUCTURE

A Tough Selling Situation:

Getting a Foot Inside the Right Door

This is indeed a tough selling situation if only because it's a prerequisite to actually having an opportunity to create an interest in your products and services. Certain doors are easy but are also the wrong doors. This chapter will help you identify the right doors as well as how to get both feet inside.

YVONNE

Yvonne Scott has been working for Sof Tech for seven months. After working in retail distribution for three years, Yvonne felt fortunate in hooking up with a small software company with a great group of people. Sof Tech wrote, edited and quality-tested user manuals for PC-based software application packages. Recently, they had been engaged to customize a bulky user manual to the specifics of its use within a large insurance company. This was a new venture for Sof Tech, but their customer awarded them a performance citation and a bonus for ahead-of-schedule completion. Andy Parcell, owner, inventor and president, wanted to repeat this success.

Andy called Yvonne into his office. She was the only one who had a sales background and an undergraduate marketing degree. "Yvonne, we need to come up with a way to capitalize on what we did for Universal Insurance. We need a new prospect . . . probably one with characteristics like Universal. What do you think?"

Yvonne said that they needed a plan, including a clear definition of the kinds of client needs that Sof Tech could satisfy. Next, they needed to select one or two companies that were likely to have those needs. Yvonne went on to suggest that they should know something concrete about any potential business before approaching it.

Yvonne talked to each employee who had worked on the Universal Insurance project. She asked each one, "What do you think Universal's problem was, and what do think are the three most important things that we did for them?" This was the start of a "needs identification" list and also helped define the product they had delivered to Universal.

Yvonne thought about what she had been asked to do—introduce a new product into an unknown market. Her mission was to find who had needs that matched what Sof Tech could do with their talent and resources. Then comes the hard part . . . getting a foot in the door!

Yvonne felt something between fear and confusion. Her short history in retail sales had not taught her about business-to-busi-

ness selling. Sof Tech was a tiny company and was informally managed. A prospective client for Sof Tech's new product would be a
large company with a complex and formal organization. Yvonne
didn't know where to start. She needed a practical crash course
about who does what in such companies. What important executive
would allow her foot in the door? Which door is the right door?
Yvonne felt stalled. She needed help or an unusual inspiration.

Salespeople often display more courage than a charging bull
and depend more on luck than the most addicted gambler.
Many salespeople will merely breeze into a new company
with no more knowledge than the location of the front
door. The following material suggests that knowledge about
the Business Management Structure (BMS) of an account is a
prerequisite for effective penetration and development of
that account. This in turn is a key prerequisite for maximiz-
ing your opportunities to attain new business. Similarly, if
you are already getting business in that account, it can become the essential ingredient for keeping it.

BMS refers to how an organization aligns itself to perform
its mission. Remember, Robert (in Chapter 2) lost National
Industrial Aid mostly because he wasn't positioned to defend
against change. He had no current knowledge of the recent
responsibility changes in his customer's organization.

Think about how much talent, time, and effort have been
invested in developing and organizing an operating structure within any company. Even that company's own employees can hardly make anything happen unless they
understand, appreciate, and use the existing structure. The
structure defines the rules of conduct, the decision-making
processes, the limits of authority, and areas of responsibility
and turf ownership. The structure we are referring to is quite
unlike the visible preciseness of an organization chart. Such
charts only hint at the real structure and its operating
mechanisms. The real structure is much more elusive and
somewhat fluid. The real structure may have to be perceived
or imagined in any particular situation.

The trick is to pick up on those characteristics that seem to influence the current shape of the structure. For example, market demand for the company's products, or a sudden sales slump, or several executive replacements may all affect the way the structure operates. These examples imply that change is required to adapt to a new course. What is the current course? Is the atmosphere optimistic? Do the executives speak to growth and new opportunities in interviews and company publications? When racing ahead, upper managers are less inhibited by the formal structure (chain of command) and are inclined to move quickly.

The professional salesperson who consistently excels will demonstrate techniques necessary to interface with the shifting nature of the prospect's Business Management Structure. This causes us to look at information that will help us grasp and use the BMS within our target accounts. (The courage of a charging bull and a little good luck will also help.)

CHARACTERIZING YOUR ACCOUNTS

It is to your advantage to understand some of the factors that have developed over time and have now resulted in the structure that is documented as their organization chart. For example, is the founder still active in the business? Has a recent merger or significant acquisition caused new management to arrive on the scene? Any of the above may have much to do about the makeup of the current structure and how it functions. Salespeople must have a good working knowledge of their account's structure if they intend to put together a doable Account Development plan. The following eight considerations will help you to understand and characterize your account.

1. *The Formal Organization.* Some organizations are rigidly hierarchical, drive all decisions and actions within chains of command, and punish disruptions or devia-

tions. Others are flexibly organized and are not too concerned about organizational structure. Some organizations are controlled by centralized authority, while others are decentralized and show strong autonomy in divisions, departments, etc. The organization's approach to formal structure will greatly affect how it buys and how you should sell.

2. *The Informal Organization.* Whatever the type of formal organization in place, people often create decision and information networks to satisfy personal needs and to get things done. Students of organization have frequently claimed that the informal organization is more important in explaining what really happens in most companies. The informal organizations reveal who works with whom, whose opinions *really* count, who trusts whom, and on whom the organization relies for its critical efforts. A salesperson who understands a company's informal organization has the insights of an insider and will be hard to beat. A sales executive once explained it this way, "In your home, guests eat in the dining room; friends eat in the kitchen."

3. *Policies versus Practices.* Most companies have developed policies and procedures that govern key functions and activities. Many policies are rigid and are followed to the letter, such as policies for creating financial statements and for hiring. Other policies may be documented and discussed in an equally thorough fashion, but are not as rigorously followed. Purchasing activity is frequently one of the activities that falls into this "semi-policy" area. Rules are often bent, informal/unofficial input is common, and executive intervention is to be expected in important procurements. Salespeople need to know how the game is played and how to focus their efforts accordingly.

4. *Problem-Solving Style.* How does a company, department, or business unit react to a big problem? What
happens if their funding is out, a key person quits, or a
big project is late? Some organizations react by isolat-
ing the troubled unit, some change its leaders, and
others send a rescue team. By understanding how a
group solves problems, you can often understand what
is behind a particular buying activity and how to position your response. For example, if they do lots of
committee studies, then you'll want to understand
their charter and who the real leader is. If the responsible executive is one who delegates most details, then
you'll need to know whom he or she depends on. Such
knowledge means that sometimes you can anticipate
solutions, and in the most ideal scenario you'll help
shape a solution.

5. *Culture.* An organization's culture visually reflects its
traditions and the personalities of key people. Culture
can often be seen in how willing to change people are,
how open to risk they are, and how carefully they try
to control communication. Organizational culture can
often be described in clusters of adjectives; i.e., rigid,
conservative, formal, traditional, cautious; or flexible,
innovative, informal, trendy, dynamic. Salespeople
with a good feeling for a customer's culture know how
to shape their proposals.

6. *Size.* The characteristics associated with size affect an
organization's Business Management Structure. The
following characteristics are usually associated differently with large and small organizations. (You can add
your own to the list.)

7. *Relationship with Customers, Suppliers.* A basic question
about any organization is, "Does it look inward or outward?" Obviously, any organization does both, but
how open a company is to the outside world is critical
to its mission and methods. Organizations that are

Characteristic	Large Organization	Small Organization
Senior Executives	Planning, direction— not involved in operations	Involved in all big decisions, hands-on
Functions	Specialists (not my job)	Everybody does everything
Policies	Thorough	Wing it
Dollars and time	Looking out 6 months to 1 year	Next payroll, today and tomorrow
Decision making	Complex, formal, slow	"Looks good, do it!"

open to the outside world aggressively seek the counsel of their customers, prospects, and suppliers. Organizations that look inward, that build barriers between themselves and the world, are unlikely to seek new ideas, and are less likely to listen to new vendors. To some degree, your chance to win new business from new accounts depends on how they view you and the rest of the outside world.

8. *Plans and Goals.* Well-run organizations make decisions that reflect clearly articulated goals and create plans that will achieve those goals. Poorly run organizations either have no goals or ignore them. As a consequence, they seldom do serious planning. If you are selling to a well-run organization, it is important that you link your efforts to their goals and plans. If your prospect's goals and plans are mere "boilerplate," you must find the other factors that are driving their effort. (If your prospect isn't doing a good job of planning, you may have an opportunity to help them refine their plans. In such a favorable situation, it's perfectly okay to keep your own best interest at the forefront.)

It is important to have current information about your business community and particularly about your customer's businesses. Keep notes on information picked up during your routine activities. Make copies of important call reports and build a customer file to keep them in. We recommend that you cut and paste important articles and keep them in the customer files. You shouldn't forget the following sources.

Outside Sources

Financial Information	General Business Information
Dun & Bradstreet	*The Wall Street Journal*
10K's	*Business Week*
Daily stock performance	*Barron's*
Annual reports	Local newspapers
Financial industry analyst report	Industry-specific journals
	Business directories

Account Sources	Other Sources
Stockholder Relations Office	Non-competing vendor's sales and service people
Public relations departments	Chamber of Commerce
Sales literature	Professional Associations
	Former Employees

Customer Sources

- Interview key customer personnel when there is *no* direct sales activity (no pressure on either of you).

- Make information courtesy calls on customer executives with your company's executives.

- Interview personnel within your own company with previous associations in your account.

FACT—REAL WORLD: No one has time to do all the above.

QUESTION—REAL WORLD: Do you make the time to do any of the above?

Some General Observations

- You will be amazed at what people will tell you if you take the time to talk and listen (the operative word is "listen") to them when there is no sale at stake.

- Think through the following questions: What added value can I bring to my account? What can I do beyond providing my product and service?

- Develop a detailed understanding of the Decision-Making Process (DMP) before a proposal is in effect; i.e., "Mr. Customer, if we were to do X, how would that happen?" (This is a "shadow" sales effort.)

- Develop a "mentor" inside your account; preferably someone close to the decision process and able to influence it.

PUTTING YOUR KNOWLEDGE TO WORK

To understand and take advantage of the client's Business Management Structure, salespeople should ask themselves the following questions about their important accounts:

1. How are buying decisions made?

2. Who makes buying decisions? Who influences them?

3. What is shaping, causing, or constraining these decisions?

4. How should we position ourselves for near-term business?

5. How should we position ourselves for long-term business?

6. How can our organization support our sales position?

7. What do I need to know to deal with competition and other account problems?

After you have done your homework and planned your initial calls, the best way to obtain expanded information and/or validation on the seven items mentioned above is to get help from within the organization. Any of these items can be carefully framed as questions that can be asked of almost any contact you may have. There are more than enough people who are willing to show how much they know about what's going on and why it's happening. Below, a salesperson makes a call on Mr. Henry. We relate that part of the conversation designed to solicit Mr. Henry's help in solving a difficult problem.

Mr. Henry, I've read the request for proposal [RFP] and we want to respond, but I'm having a real problem. It's not apparent to me just what problems are being solved by the RFP. And, because I don't understand the problem, any creativity I could offer or any of our product options or custom modifications that could be beneficial to your company aren't going to be considered. Can you give me some direction so that we can do our best job for you?

You can juggle the words around anyway you like, but there are always three elements. First, you make a statement to set the stage: I'm aware of; I've been told; I have heard that perhaps; I have tried; and so on. Next, you make a modest statement that positions you as one who needs help in order to make a contribution: I don't understand; I'm a little confused; I feel as though; I only want a chance, but;

and so on. And, finally, you ask Mr. Henry to share with you: Can you?; Will you?; Please straighten me out; I want to represent my company in the best way, but; and so on.

The technique seldom fails. If you want to test it in a no-loss situation, try it on a nonbusiness subject in any non-customer environment. There is a subtle flattery here that seems to force a response that justifies the compliment. Here is one more example from the same conversation:

> *Mr. Henry, another reason I specifically wanted to see you today relates to a business problem I have. I want to do the things in your company that give me an opportunity to earn the respect given only to worthy suppliers. My problem is that I can't find a starting place. I'm told, in so many words, that my company will never even get on the short list . . . I don't know why. I can't give up, anymore than you would want a salesperson representing your company to just throw in the towel. My company, like yours, has good products; but, Mr. Henry, I'm at a loss and don't know what to do. I need advice, and I wanted to see you and ask for some knowledgeable direction. Can you help?*

This last example relates to items 4 and 5 from the above list. Believe us, the odds of getting both advice and direction are good. Additionally, you've got a perfect open gate for a follow-up call, and you've established the initial phase for developing an internal advocate.

THE ORGANIZATIONAL INHABITANTS

Organizational inhabitants are mostly regular people just like you. Some of them stay that way even after they go to work each day. Others act differently from eight to five, perhaps because organizational expectations and associated circumstances force the change. In many companies, people are expected to act a certain way depending on the nature of their job, the extent of their responsibilities, and their job title. It matters little that most would deny they succumb to such insignificant trappings; the fact is that they do.

Our experiences allow us to place the inhabitants into five broad categories. These categories are most applicable to larger organizations such as the Fortune 2000.

- The Highest of the High

- Executives

- Middle Management

- Specialist Groups

- The Workers

The Highest of the High

Nobody knows fully what these people do. You and I don't care because they're so far removed from the operative side of what's going on, they make no difference to us. If there are two parts to a company, one being the part that makes things, brings in revenue, and employs people, then these people must be in charge of the *other* part. They think of the company as a person in that it has a personality, an image, a net worth, and is a responsible citizen. The company can be an extension of themselves. They have projects and goals that keep them busy. Some of these may even relate to the business at hand. They use resources from the other part of the company to help achieve these projects and goals. They are in demand as speakers, contributors, and as board members for other companies. They sometimes appoint executives in an attempt to remain bonded to the functional part of the company.

Executives

We suggest that there are three categories of executives: top executives, staff executives, and operating executives. All three categories can be very useful to the professional salesperson who has an Account Development Strategy.

Top executives will often be in charge of one or more of the company's businesses. The demands on them and the challenges given to them can be enormous. They have risen above the specifics of their backgrounds to become pragmatic generalists. They are constantly on the prowl for information. They are always in a meeting . . . which they called. They are decisive. They are cool and always under control. They are driven by numbers that are expressions of their goals and responsibilities. If they find something broken, or that may break, they fix it with a word. They manage to operate in spite of the coercion and impediments that rain down from the highest of the high. If they are really good at what they do, there is little upward mobility available to them within the same company.

Staff executives do work for other executives. They can be a good source of information about what's going on. They do lots of committee and task force work. They can be laid back because they have time. The good ones can be influential on top executives and operating executives. People lower in the organization generally think that they have more power than they really do. They like to think things over. By definition, they are not decisive, and it is difficult to measure their performance. Top executives give them assignments relating to matters that don't need to be decided yet. Operating executives give them assignments they don't feel are worthwhile dealing with anyway. It's the operating executives' way of shelving nonessential projects or appearing to work on something that just interferes with the real job at hand.

Good salespeople find it relatively easy to get appointments with staff executives. Use them to gather information. Don't try to get them to make something happen for you. They can become candidates for a position with the highest of the high.

Operating or *line executives* run the businesses. They operate under fire. They too are decisive and are most closely attuned to the nuts and bolts. They may not delegate well and can burn out fast. There is no place to pass the buck.

They are only interested in meeting the business objectives and will do whatever is necessary in this regard. They can appear to be cruel and will show little or no mercy where performance is an issue. They work the longest hours of all employees. They are accessible, but only for a very good cause. They do not allow second chances. They give no forgiveness and expect none for themselves. They are good people, but it may not be obvious. They leave to pursue other business opportunities.

Middle Management

Middle management runs the business on a day-to-day basis. They hire and fire and can have frequent direct customer contacts. They bend and break company procedures as a routine course of survival. They operate under expense and revenue or cost-transfer budgets. Many are in training to become operating executives. They take risks because they don't have the time to do otherwise. They have no use for staff executives and will go to great extremes to avoid any interest or interference from them. The good ones are both visible and vulnerable. They are the proving ground for good plans handed down from above as well as those that could never work anyway. Future line executives come from the ranks of successful middle managers, and future staff executives come from those who shot themselves in the foot.

Specialist Groups

Specialist groups include the legal department, the advertising group, personnel, and so on. These generally serve multiple businesses. Their operating costs are customarily passed on to the businesses they serve. Certain of their members may be specifically assigned to a business segment, and they often become very knowledgeable about some facets of that business. Top executives use these groups to avoid unnecessary risks and to provide consistency. Line executives put up with them to avoid backside exposure and organizational conflicts. Middle management's prevalent view is that the specialist groups are bottlenecks. They will interpret or define work situations in such a fashion that the specialists' charters are not applicable. When this is successful, then they don't have to put up with them.

These specialists are reluctant to talk to outsiders about what they are doing because it commonly involves events that have not happened yet. Even so, these people will usually surrender to careful cultivation and can be a source of knowledge for the understanding and supportive salesperson (personnel excepted). They generally do not move up, down, or sideways within the organization. Their future is probably with some other company. They are easy to see and will talk about their charter and the mechanics of what they do.

Workers

The workers may know how your products are really functioning in their area. It's wise to get good report cards from them, so reasonable account service calls should be made. Their reports (good or bad) can give you good reasons to support your request for a middle management appointment. These people are glad that you care. They don't have much control over their time, so you should respect their position.

As we move down the "company size" scale, our five inhabitant categories begin to change characteristics. The highest of the high slowly disappear and are replaced by owners, partners, and/or stockholders. The executive groups change into a small but effective core group who think of themselves as operating managers. Staff executives disappear completely, as there are no projects beyond those that can have an immediate effect on the business. The specialist groups become extinct because such needs are subcontracted to small special purpose companies. The personnel function is reduced to keeping track of required numbers and is likely to be a part of the payroll function. Middle managers become skilled supervisory workers. Workers begin to take on a higher profile and have greater responsibilities coupled with more access to the management ranks.

Special Inhabitants

We cannot recall ever being a part of an organization, or becoming familiar with a customer organization, that did not have some *special* people. Our definition of special is this: They are committed to their company and to their jobs. They work hard. They are creative and well-informed. They can display an open mind, and they are interested in new things. They know how to use their organization's resources and how to avoid getting wrapped around the axle. They don't take advantage; they just get things done. They respect those upper managers who deserve respect and loyalty, and they commend and give greater responsibilities to those subordinates who have earned it. They are extremely fair, but one cannot easily take advantage of this. They are candid. They generally don't agree that the way it's always been done is the best way.

When you find one of these people operating in the segment of the Business Management Structure in which you have an interest, try very hard to make contact with them. Your story has to be very good and very pertinent. You will excite them with ideas and concepts but will eventually have to back it up with reality. After your presentation, these people will tell you exactly what they want you to do next. It's a high-risk call, because they may tell you to disappear . . . forever. The good part is that you will know.

YVONNE'S SOLUTION

Yvonne selected a company for her product and began her search for the right door. She prepared a strong interest statement designed to get an appointment to enter that door based on the following information:

- What they did for Universal Insurance

- What it meant in terms of benefits

- Other options they could have selected

- Products offered

- Characteristics of a company that would benefit from their products

- What their story is and who will listen to it

Initial calls on training departments or MIS groups were considered high risk or a downright mistake. Both groups would contend that they already had a back-burner plan to make life easier for all those employees using PC-based application programs. Additionally, neither group was in a position to fund a nonforecasted activity.

Through her research, Yvonne discovered an executive at her prospect company who was also on the board at Universal Insurance. She decided that he was someone who could cause a large front-end expenditure to happen even though it wasn't budgeted anywhere. She made an appointment to tell her story. She was correct in her assumption that he would listen and understand abstract and indirect benefits, such as job enrichment, and the value of outsourcing such a project as she proposed.

Many salespeople start selling at the wrong door. The two reasons are that they take the first open door available or that they don't do enough research to *know* which door is the right door. Understanding the Business Management Structure will help you find the right executive's door. When you're inside, and if your story has executive level appeals, the worst thing that can happen is that you'll be redirected to a *decision-making* subordinate.

CHAPTER 4

UNDERSTANDING PERSONALITY TYPES

A Tough Selling Situation:

The Prospect Won't Listen and
Gets Defensive

*You were given the time on the prospect's calendar,
but now he or she seems to want to take it back. You're
trying to make your call sound like a conversation, but the
prospect appears to want a confrontation. Did you say
something wrong or inappropriate? It's a frustrating selling problem that seems to get worse as your sales call
continues.*

HARRY

Harry had called high and got a good hearing from Fred Parker, Executive Vice President of Manufacturing. Mr. Parker had then referred Harry to Chad Donaldson, the plant manager and senior engineer assigned to quality control. Chad knew that Harry had talked to Parker but didn't seem to be impressed.

Harry started talking about the leadership role his company, Drive Engineering Inc., held in the belt drive industry. Chad said he was familiar with Harry's company, but didn't consider them industry leaders, at least not for the past four or five years. Chad had a determined set to his jaw. Harry remembered that Mr. Parker had not questioned DEI'S leadership position, but Chad planted his stake firmly and never backed off. He had even quietly asked Harry to prove the leading role statement!

Harry assumed that every salesperson said that their company, their products and service, and their price performance were the best. Wasn't that what customers were used to hearing and what they expected to hear? It wasn't supposed to be an issue. You had to say that because all the other salespeople were saying it.

Harry pushed ahead with all the emphasis he could muster. He named several companies that used his products, but that didn't seem to budge Chad. The guy just sat there! Harry could feel his patience wearing thin. He mentioned that DEI had gone into the International Marketplace this year, and Chad said that he hoped they did well . . . and that was all that he said.

Chad then said that he had to break away for a quality meeting, and Harry never did get another shot at the leadership issue. He gave Chad a copy of DEI's current ad that was running in several industry journals touting the fact that DEI was a leading belt drive manufacturer.

Harry felt that he and Mr. Parker had hit it off well together and that Parker would see him again. Maybe Parker could refer him to someone else. If not, Harry would have another shot at Chad. Maybe Chad was just having a bad day.

When you are calling high, you must also assume a "one shot, best shot" approach. There is a discernible difference between listeners; you must be able to tailor and customize both your style and your material to their way of taking in information. Gathering advance information about your audience will help you to more effectively target your presentations. Fortunately, there are also ways you can read your audience on the fly and adjust your message in midstream. Recognizing and understanding your approach techniques is the key. The information in this chapter will help you to analyze yourself and other parties in your business environment, and then adjust your approach to fit the combination of personalities.

People relate to each other in three basic ways: They can move against (Dominance), away (Detachment), or toward (Relational). Everybody relates in all three ways, but most people are primarily dominant, detached, or relational. Descriptions of the extremes of each personality type help us to see the pattern; but remember that very few people have all the characteristics of these extreme types. We will discuss how each type of person positions themselves in the communication process and then suggest ways that you might use to talk and deal with them.

DOMINANT PEOPLE

Dominant people always want to take control. They are extremely competitive and must win at everything. Business, golf, even cocktail parties are contests. They need to make more money, play better golf, and "score more points" than their friends at a party. Status consciousness is a natural part of their personality. When they meet strangers, they want to know, "Am I better than they are?" Do I make more money, own a larger house, have a lower handicap, and so on? They are ambitious, tough, aggressive, manipulative, overbearing, closed-minded, anti-intellectual, and insensitive. Since everything is a contest, they cannot afford to think about abstract subjects or other people's feelings. It would distract their attention from the only goal that matters—WINNING. Since winning is so important, some dominant people cut corners. They would rather not lie or cheat because it taints their victory, but a tainted victory is infinitely better than a defeat.

They are fiercely independent and individualistic. Taking orders, accepting advice, or following procedures is a kind of defeat. They therefore insist on doing things their way, and may even go out of the way to break the rules. They tend to distrust people. They know that they will do anything to win and therefore assume that other people want to take advantage of them. They are afraid of losing, weakness in themselves, and dependency on other people. Some of them even ruin their health trying to deny their weaknesses. For example, some fifty-year-old men get heart attacks from playing five sets of tennis or trying to prove that they "can work these young kids under the table."

When they meet other dominant people, it may be total war. Both feel "It is either him or me, and it is not going to be him." They absolutely dominate relational people. Relational people naturally accept a submissive role, and the dominant person despises and bullies them. In fact, some dominant people deliberately surround themselves with people they can easily push around. Detached people frustrate them. They cannot stand being ignored, and want to grab the other person by the collar and yell, "Come out of your ivory tower and fight like a real person!" Their aggressiveness frightens the other person, causing further withdrawal. Ultimately, the dominant person gives up and goes looking for "my kind of people."

Dominant Salespeople

Dominance can be a real plus in the world of selling, and nearly all good negotiators have a liberal amount of it. You must want to score! However, excessive dominance will reduce your effectiveness. Carefully assess the following observations about dominant salespeople and contemplate how they might influence or otherwise turn a deal:

1. Their general approach is competitive and high pressure. They assume that people do not want to buy into a deal and that their job is to wear down resistance with arguments, pressure, and just plain tenacity.

2. Planning is generally ignored or done superficially. They want to be a part of the action, not sit around thinking.

3. The opening statement is the first shot in the battle. They try to take control immediately to show that they are the boss.

4. Diagnosis is generally superficial and may not occur at all. They assume that they know what the prospect needs.

5. Information is usually well organized and hard hitting. However, since the diagnosis was poor, the interpretation may not relate directly to the prospect's problems and interests.

6. Objections are rarely analyzed, and the answers to them are often long and aimless. Instead of clarifying concerns, they try to overwhelm with arguments and pressure.

7. The close is their greatest strength. Getting the deal is the ultimate victory, losing it the ultimate defeat. So they become inflexible and continue to pound away at their original position.

8. Records are seldom organized and updated. The impression is that they got all the information the first time around.

9. Follow-ups are rare and superficial. Once they have won, they want to move on to the next battle. If they lose, they won't return to the scene of the crime, so to speak.

10. Winning is so important that they will even take unpleasant actions to increase their production. They dislike analyzing themselves, but dislike losing even more. For example, if one can prove that a particular deal was lost because an objection was not understood, they will try in the future to clarify objections before answering them.

Dominant Prospects

These people distrust anyone trying to sell them on a deal and are afraid that they will be exploited and defeated. However, many of them actually like having to go through the process. They are stimulated by the battle of wits with the dominant ones and enjoy bullying the others. Their hidden questions are: Are you good enough to get my business? Are you a top producer? Do you earn as much as I do? Are you tough enough to slug it out with me? Their status consciousness makes them want to deal with the top people. They want the manager or even the president to handle their business.

They generally want to deal with people who are dominant enough to earn their respect. They dislike and avoid detached people. They despise and abuse relational people, but occasionally "throw them a bone" to build up their own egos.

While your selling personality is important when calling on the dominant prospect, you will be most effective if you will practice the advice given in the following list:

1. The most effective approach is smooth dominance. You must prove that you are tough and competent, without actually defeating them.

2. Your plans should be thorough. They love to catch errors and may pick you apart if you are poorly prepared, or if the deal is not presented well.

3. Your opening should be brisk and businesslike, but not threatening. Build rapport by showing respect for their importance and time.

4. Diagnosis is fairly easy. They generally like to talk, and are inhibited only by their distrust of you. If you ask a couple of open-ended questions and listen actively to the answers, they will usually tell you what you need to know. They are really starved for understanding because many people are too frightened to try to understand them.

5. Your information should be brief, well organized, and absolutely correct. Never stretch the truth with them; you will just reinforce their natural cynicism. Do not try to cover every possible situation. They are impatient listeners and would rather develop new ideas in a back-and-forth manner.

6. Analyze their objections carefully before you answer. They bitterly resent answers that show you did not understand them. What right do you have to ignore their ideas? Your answers should not directly contradict them or cause them to lose face.

7. Your conclusions should be direct and forceful, but should never seem to be a demand for surrender. Lay out the facts, then appeal to their decisiveness and independence.

8. When the deal is made, get away as quickly as possible. They may be so uneasy about their "defeat" that they interpret innocent remarks as signs of gloating. If they do so, kiss the deal good-bye.

9. Any follow-up should be brief and businesslike. Show them that you are giving them first-class treatment, but show your respect for their time by getting directly to the point.

DETACHED PEOPLE

Detached people are more comfortable with things, ideas, or numbers than they are with people. They distrust people, particularly ones who try to dominate or get close to them. They do not understand emotions and try to avoid them. They suppress their own emotions and ignore other people's. They are shy, aloof, impersonal, and uncommunicative.

They generally like order and predictability. They carefully control themselves and prefer controlled, predictable environments. Their desks, homes and checkbooks are arranged perfectly, and they can be severely upset by minor deviations from their customary routines.

They are independent, but in a different manner than dominant people. They have even less need for people, but they do need and like rules. They want to be alone, but they do not want to flaunt authority. They readily accept the impersonal authority of rules and procedures, but avoid people who attempt to control them directly.

They are open-minded about impersonal issues. They like facts and logic, and pride themselves on their objectivity. If one challenges their position, they do not respond angrily. They try to look at the facts objectively and will change their position if the data require it. They generally work in fields that require objective, impersonal analysis, such as chemistry, physics, engineering, accounting, statistics, and management sciences. They enjoy this kind of work and are most comfortable with the kind of people who enter such fields.

They are afraid of closeness, dependency, and unpredictability. In fact, a major reason for avoiding people is that they are not as predictable as numbers or machines. Their relationships with other detached people are comfortable, but distant. They enjoy each other's minds, and neither make demands on the other. They feel contempt, fear, hostility, and anger toward relational people. They regard them as illogical and emotional, the two most deadly sins in their book. They resent their demands on them and are frightened by their attempts to get close to them. They respond by running away. They are even more negative toward dominant people. They regard them as illogical, emotional bullies and avoid them completely.

Detached Salespeople

Most salespeople could use more detachment. It would help them to analyze the actions of the other person and to develop a winning approach. Very few salespeople and dealmakers are primarily detached, and hardly any of them are extreme. The primarily detached do not like the give-and-take involved in a business deal, and those who try generally do not succeed. The very detached personality simply cannot cope with the emotional elements of the typical sales environment. Nevertheless, we will describe the extremely detached person's approach:

1. Their general approach is logical, fact-oriented, impersonal, and low pressure. They essentially try to convert business solutions into an abstract, intellectual exercise. They assume that people will buy into the solution that best fits their needs and will ignore the irrational factors that influence so many decisions.

2. Their planning is generally excellent, but they often spend too much time on it. They would rather work on their plans than talk to people.

3. Their opening statements are impersonal and lack attempts to build rapport. They want to relate to the other person as if they were both computers, and they concentrate exclusively on the objective facts. This approach turns off many people.

4. Their diagnosis of objective facts is thorough and occasionally brilliant. They listen well, try to get all the facts, and take the time to organize these facts into a coherent picture. However, some people dislike their coldness and refuse to tell them anything. Instead of recognizing their own inadequacies, the detached person concludes that others are illogical and tends to avoid them. They also do not learn anything about the other's psychological needs and problems. They relate only to impersonal facts.

5. They present information in a factual and logical manner, but it lacks emotional appeal. Their presentations also tend to be much too long. They try to present the complete picture, including all the minor facts.

6. They listen carefully to concerns and provide all the information they can. However, they cannot handle stalls or hidden objections. Stalling is so illogical that they can neither understand it nor use pressure on procrastinators. They cannot probe for hidden objections because they cannot understand their emotional basis. Hard objections are almost impossible for them to handle because they are forced to face unpleasant facts.

7. Closing is their greatest weakness. They assume that the other party will make a logical decision and, therefore, they hesitate to ask for a conclusion. If they ask once and are turned down, they rarely ask again. They also hesitate to use "gimmicks" such as the forced choice or tacit approval techniques.

8. Their proposals are written perfectly. Every detail is correct.

9. Their follow-ups are meticulous, but impersonal. They analyze events thoroughly and see that their commitments are on time. They do not, however, develop a

personal relationship with the customer or prospect. They can't believe that more information and aggressive persistence would be necessary or even helpful.

10. They work hard in technical training courses, but dislike and avoid sales courses. They want to improve in the areas they have already mastered, but will not work on their real weaknesses. They are not motivated to improve their techniques or to become more sensitive to the emotions of others.

Detached Prospects

Detached prospects distrust and dislike people who are clearly in the business of selling something. They regard the entire sales process as an imposition and do their best to avoid it. They feel that they are objective and informed enough to analyze their own problems. They want to put out a bid and then call it a day.

Their major explicit question is: What are the facts? Their hidden questions are: Are you logical and objective, or would you manipulate me? Will you give me the facts I need to make a decision without intruding on my privacy? They generally buy into a deal from detached people. They dislike the other types, particularly the dominant ones. They hate to be pushed and pressured.

Selling to prospects in this group is a challenge and demands high levels of logic and concentration. It can also be a test of the professional's ability to stay on track throughout the call. The following list should be your guideline for achieving success with your detached prospects:

1. Your most effective approach is impersonal, logical, and factual. Let the facts speak for themselves. Keep your personality out of the interaction.

2. Your plans should be even more thorough than they were for dominant prospects. You need to know all the facts.

3. Your opening should be very brief and impersonal. Minimize the social amenities; say exactly why you have called.

4. Your major diagnostic problem is to get the other person to talk. You must say what information you need and why you need it, then ask specific questions to get it. Keep control of the conversation, but do not dominate it. Just make sure that the other person realizes that you know exactly what you are doing.

5. Your explanations should be detailed, impersonal, and factual; and you should have extensive supporting material.

6. Make sure that you understand exactly what an objection means, then answer it impersonally, factually, and logically. If you suspect a hidden objection, answer it indirectly; do not openly discuss emotional issues.

7. Seeking agreement should be low pressure and logical. These people hate to be pushed. Instead, show that the most logical action is suggested. Balance sheet conclusions are particularly effective.

8. The final deal or proposal must be documented completely and properly. These people resent poor paperwork so much that they will occasionally kill a deal because of it.

9. Your follow-up should be thorough, but do not make contact unless you have something definite to discuss. If you have only routine information, a memo is better than a personal contact. Never call just to say, "Hello."

RELATIONAL PEOPLE

Relational people really need other people's love, acceptance, understanding, and approval. They are warm, friendly, and sincerely interested in other people. They enjoy all forms of social gatherings, but do not try to dominate them. They are happy being part of a group. They are good listeners and sensitive to other people's moods and personalities. They care about people and want to understand them. They are cooperative and compliant. They may go along with other people's ideas only because they want to be liked. They are givers. They want to help people, especially ones who reward them with gratitude and affection.

All of these characteristics make them popular, but they are still not sure that other people really care about them. They therefore constantly ask for reassurance. These demands reduce people's respect for them and can become an intolerable strain. After implying that "I really like you" several times, people don't care to keep doing it. But their need for reassurance is so great that they continue to ask for it. These requests can become so exhausting that the other person withdraws. The withdrawal increases the insecurity and requests for reassurance, which causes further withdrawal. This escalating spiral continues until the relationship breaks down.

Their insecurity makes them easy to exploit and manipulate. They go along with suggestions, even when they suspect they are being taken. They are loyal to people who do not deserve it. They are intensely afraid of being alone, of rejection, and of all forms of conflict (including competition). They are also frightened by all forms of hostility, especially their own. They want to believe that they feel warmly toward everyone. Jealousy is a serious problem. They become jealous and hostile toward anyone who threatens to come between them and the people they like, but feel guilty about their own feelings.

They generally relate well to other relational people. Both satisfy the other's needs, but both of them may suspect that they are giving more than the other. They allow dominant people to bully and exploit them. However, at times their resentment becomes so great that they cannot suppress it; then they lash out in extremely destructive ways. Detached people really frustrate them. They want to get close, but the other person keeps pulling away. They chase them for a while, then give up and look for friendlier types.

Relational Salespeople

Some relational characteristics are useful to a salesperson. Most people are receptive to someone they like, someone who really cares about them. Relational people can often become dependent upon, and easily controlled by others. Excessive dependency is a severe liability. They risk rejection every time they make a call, and every time they ask for a decision. Highly relational people simply cannot afford that risk. Therefore, they do not make enough calls; they talk only to people who are friendly, and their calls are often social occasions rather than genuine attempts to line up new business opportunities.

Relational salespeople do well in "sales support" roles. Many do not enjoy the competitive aspect of selling against quotas and lack enthusiasm for company sales campaigns. The following list highlights most of the selling difficulties experienced by those in this group:

1. Their general approach is to make people like them. They assume that people give their business to people they like. Unfortunately, their extreme need to be liked causes others to back off.

2. Their plans focus on the person, not the business opportunity. They concentrate on learning how to establish the best possible relationship and minimize the need for other types of information.

3. Their openings are warm, friendly, and much too long. They enjoy small talk and are afraid that getting down to business will harm their relationship (although the opposite is often the case).

4. During the diagnosis they get a lot of information, but much of it is irrelevant. People like to talk to sympa-

thetic listeners, but the conversation wanders all over the place.

5. Their communications tend to be vague and overly long. They do not get directly to the point, and they may not discuss important topics that they perceive could offend or annoy.

6. They listen carefully to objections, and their sympathetic concern makes it easy for prospects to raise hidden objections. However, their answers are too long and too vague, and they cannot use the pressure needed to overcome stalls and hard objections.

7. Closing is their greatest weakness. They simply cannot push for anything that they need or want. In fact, they sometimes do not even ask for feedback, and rarely ask more than once. They are afraid that asking for something specific will change a pleasant chat into an unpleasant confrontation.

8. They also spend too much time chatting after the agreement or close. It is much more pleasant to continue talking about the deal than to contact someone new who might reject them.

9. Their follow-ups are generally excellent. They sincerely care about the other party's interest and work hard to see that they are protected. They also contact people that they know, frequently and cheerfully.

10. They cooperate superficially with training efforts, but resist working on their real weaknesses. Rejection is so painful to them that it is almost impossible to get them to reach out and prospect for new opportunities.

Relational Prospects

Relational people are the easiest ones to call on. They will not reject you openly, and many of them like talking business with a seller, especially friendly ones. Their hidden questions are: Do you sincerely care about me? Do you like me? Are you just being nice to get the business your way? If the answers are no, no, yes, they'll still talk and listen because they want to try to change the answers to yes, yes, no!

They generally conclude a transaction only with people they like. Some of them actually accept inferior products, or pay higher prices, to give business to old friends, young people who need the business, and so on. The nine items listed below assure your selling success with these prospects:

1. The most effective approach is friendly dominance. Convince them of your sincerity, but firmly control the interview. They need to be pushed and want you to do so—if they believe that you are pushing them for their own good.

2. Your plans do not have to be detailed. They are charitable people who will forgive or even ignore actions that would irritate other types. If possible, learn something about their personal interest.

3. Your communications should be warm, friendly, and unhurried. Talk about their personal interest; point out similarities between the two of you. Do not rush them. Remember, with them it is important to be liked, so show them that you are their kind of person.

4. The diagnosis may not be as brief or organized as you would like. You may be frustrated by irrelevant comments, but you cannot afford to show it. Do not try to hurry the process with a series of closed-ended questions. Gently direct the conversation toward the areas you must explore, but accept occasional detours as unavoidable.

5. Your information should be brief, but not coldly businesslike. Communicate both your professionalism and your friendliness.

6. Listen carefully and probe gently for hidden objections. These people hesitate to say things that might offend you.

7. Your close should be forceful, but friendly. These people are indecisive and do not mind being pushed by people they trust.

8. Take your time after getting agreement. Do not appear eager to break things off. Chat for a few minutes when your business is completed.

9. The follow-up is most important, particularly its social aspects. Call frequently, even if you have nothing important to say. If you prove that you are not one of those people who gets a deal and runs away, you may have a loyal partner forever.

Table 4.1, Understanding Customer Personalities, provides a brief review of the interactive aspects of sales situations between dominant, detached, and relational personality types.

ANALYZING YOUR OWN PERSONALITY

Each extreme personality type has a characteristic pattern of strengths and weaknesses and is most effective with certain types of people. You should therefore decide how dominant, detached, and relational you are, then plan to exploit your strengths, compensate for your weaknesses, and concentrate on people who are most receptive to your characteristics and ways of doing things.

If you are primarily dominant, soften your general approach, particularly during opening comments; don't try to overwhelm people. Spend more time on planning and diagnosis. Listen more carefully and look for hidden problems and confusion. Follow up and show a more personal interest. If possible, concentrate on dominant and relational people.

TABLE 4.1—UNDERSTANDING CUSTOMER PERSONALITIES

	DOMINANT	DETACHED	RELATIONAL
Common reaction:	Let's fight	Avoidance	Welcome
Hidden question:	Are you good?	Are you logical?	Do you care?
You need to approach me by:	Showing me you're confident and prepared	Showing me logic and accuracy	Understanding and relating to me
Prepare:	For objections and pressure	To support technical accuracy	To create a warm relationship
Opening statement:	Assertive; advantages and benefits	Facts	Warm and sincere
Diagnosis:	Show respect for my story	Be sure you understand my story	Let me tell you my story
Presentation:	Brief, accurate, hard hitting	Factual and logical	Personalized
Objections based on:	Concepts and biases	Features and details	Fears and feelings
Buys if:	Believes you are a winner	Solution is logical	Trusts you

If you are primarily detached, be more forceful and show some caring for the other's interests and problems. Your openings should be longer and friendlier, your information shorter and harder hitting. Probe for hidden concerns; do not respond just to the logical reasons for stalling. Most important, ask repeatedly for agreement and carefully check your progress. Since these actions are unnatural and uncomfortable for you, stay involved with products and services that require an analytic approach and concentrate on detached people as often as you can.

If you are primarily relational, try to be more forceful and analytic. Stop worrying so much about whether people like you; remember that trying too hard for acceptance actually costs you respect and new business. Plan more carefully, make your openings shorter and more businesslike; keep the diagnosis closer to the purpose of your call, present your case more forcefully, and remember to check your progress repeatedly.

The questionnaire illustrated in Table 4.2 is in a forced-choice format. Circle the one word or phrase in each line that best fits you. For example, if you are oriented toward both people and facts, but are more oriented toward people, you would circle "people-oriented." When you have completed the questionnaire, compute your score by counting the number of circles in each column, then multiplying by 5. Your score for all three columns combined should be 100. The score for each column is the approximate emphasis of that characteristic. For example, if your scores were Dominance = 30, Detachment = 35, and Relational = 35, you are fairly well-balanced. On the other hand, if Dominance = 75, Detachment = 20, and Relational = 5, you are obviously extremely dominant, and not at all relational.

UNDERSTANDING IS YOUR ADVANTAGE

It has been said a million times that "you never get a second chance to make a first impression." There is truth in that. Using the illustration in Table 4.3, if you've diagnosed yourself as leaning heavily toward the dominant side and have assessed your prospect as being the detached kind of person then you must take advantage of the knowledge that this person will likely have you tagged as pushy. Therefore, you

TABLE 4.2—PERSONALITY ASSESSMENT QUESTIONNAIRE

DOMINANT	DETACHED	RELATIONAL
Attacks	Withdraws	Approaches
Money and power oriented	Fact-oriented	People-oriented
Aggressive	Objective	Friendly
Distrusting	Cool	Trusting
Insensitive	Indifferent	Sensitive
Afraid of losing	Afraid of closeness	Afraid of rejection
Needs to be strong	Needs to be alone	Needs to be accepted
Selfish	Uninvolved	Self-sacrificing
Rule breaker	Rule follower	Rule bender
Doesn't listen	Listens only for facts	Listens for emotions and facts
Enjoys selling	Dislikes the emotional aspects	Hurt by prospect's rejection
Closed-minded	Open-minded only about facts	Open-minded about people
Comfortable with winners	Not comfortable with people	Comfortable with nice people
Tough	Analytic	Tender
Competitive	Aloof	Cooperative
Talker	Thinker	Listener
Likes sports	Likes reading	Likes reading
Dominates sessions	Concentrates on the facts	Likes me
Fast conclusions	Let facts speak for themselves	Won't impose a conclusion
Few details	Considers only the issues	Hears all the problems
Circles _____	_____	_____
× Five _____	_____	_____

**TABLE 4.3—PROSPECT'S PERCEPTION OF
SALES REPRESENTATIVES**

SALES TYPE	DOMINANT PROSPECT	DETACHED PROSPECT	RELATIONAL PROSPECT
Dominant	Competitive, smooth	Illogical, pushy	Pushy and insincere
Detached	Distant—won' t compete	Comfortable but distant	Distant—doesn't like them
Relational	Weak and submissive	Emotional, not accurate	Great

are well advised to come on slowly and with logical ideas and discussions.

It doesn't pay to have an extreme personality. Fortunately, almost no one is that way. Even so, we all seem to lean in one direction more than another. It is useful to assess ourselves in this regard as well as those people with whom we communicate and do business. Whatever the subject, your opinions and points are going to have more impact when you have made an effort to understand and play to the other's mood and personality.

The information contained in this chapter is extremely important and also a tad complex. You will probably want to refer to this information frequently for a quick review of how the nuances of personalities can be combined to form a dynamic sales relationship. In anticipation of this, we have developed a summary in outline form that can be found in the Appendix.

HARRY'S SOLUTION

Harry told his office mate, Helen Marie, about his call on Chad Donaldson and she agreed that he sounded like a jerk. Aside, Helen Marie giggled and told him that she wasn't surprised that he got kicked out. Harry said, "It's not funny, Helen Marie, that account could have lots of potential business for me."

Helen Marie explained the differences between dominant, detached, and relational personality types and urged Harry to understand their importance in interacting with prospects in a selling situation. She encouraged him to analyze his own personality type so he could understand his role in the relationship.

Harry took Helen Marie's advice and decided that Chad definitely had "detached" characteristics—he was analytic, a thinker, listened only for facts, and was cold. With Helen Marie's help, he figured out that his own personality type fell into the dominant category. Once he understood how he could adjust his own personality to be more in tune with prospects, he felt confident he could work with Chad in the future.

Harry pulled some product test results from the office information file. From the competitive evaluation file, he made copies of several positive comparisons. One gem was written by an independent testing firm that ranked his product among the top four. There were several graphic illustrations that could be dressed up using the PC. Harry looked at what he had assembled and felt convinced that the facts would support his statement that DEI was a leader in the field.

Chad was reluctant to see Harry again, but finally agreed under the condition that Harry had what he said that he had. Harry had prepared carefully for this call. He steeled himself to be a listener. He would present the factual product information slowly and take Chad through it step by step. He would be patient and let Chad conclude that DEI had moved ahead and was now among the leaders. The facts would speak for themselves. The close would follow a 10-minute video that showed how DEI chemistry was extending belt life in severely polluted manufacturing environments.

The video suggested that test usage could prove noteworthy cost savings.

During the call, Harry confirmed that Chad was a classic detached type. He noted that Chad did everything on cue. After the film, Chad said that he would like to see and hold several belts with the XJH chemical coatings and that they might be interested in installing a couple of dozen in their more difficult environments. He agreed to pay for them. And Harry learned the value of understanding personality types.

CHAPTER 5

POWER COMMUNICATIONS

A Tough Selling Situation:
Dealing with Negative Perceptions

If your customer, or prospective customer, has a negative mind-set about you, your product, or your company, you must immediately address it. Should you go through a lengthy sales process only to discover the negative perception at decision time, you may have to start all over. In any event, you will need strong arguments and power communications to change mind-sets.

SCOTT

Scott's company manufactured industrial fastening devices that were used across several industries engaged in medium to heavy manufacturing. His company, Seaboard Metals, had fallen on hard times lately and a "cash poor" indictment had found its way into print in many newspapers and some industry journals. Some follow-up stories reported that the company was floundering and that it was up for sale.

Scott was already picking up vibes of concern here and there in his accounts. His buyers needed assurance that Seaboard Metals could continue to meet their needs over the long haul. He was doing his best, but could see the doubts and could feel things slipping away.

The final blow came in the Sunday newspaper's business section. The union membership drafted an article of concern about Seaboard Metals and said that they were demanding two seats on the Board of Directors. The article went on to say that a confidential union source had said that the union was prepared to make a substantial investment in Seaboard Metals if management would guarantee that any sale would be subject to the union's concurrence. The source also said that there was no imminent threat of a strike against Seaboard.

Seaboard's president issued a company-wide memo to reassure employees that Seaboard was healthy enough to withstand and overcome their current difficulties. The memo included specifics to support his position and ended by noting that over their 42 years, they had overcome similar tough times.

Scott knew that all of this would be negative news to his customers. There would be discussions about risk and consequences. He would have to hit these negative perceptions about the fate of Seaboard head on.

Because we are people who sell, we have to carefully assess just how good and how effective our overall communications really are. Success in this setting is determined by the frequency with which we are able to achieve our objective. If you usually get what you want, it might be that you've set very low expectations for your communication objective. If your objectives have been good solid ones, and you most often achieve them, or make a significant step toward your goals, you are positioned to fine-tune an asset that you already have.

While thinking about our communications, it is important that we narrow the playing field so that we escape the broad or general application of communication techniques and skills: classroom grammar, speech classes, vocabulary extension, and writing skills. We suspect that while you might benefit by improving those areas, you also do well enough to get by.

Our single concern is to help you do your best as you create and carry out your Account Development plans. Therefore, our brand of communications is targeted toward your direct contacts with important business managers. Our communication thrust is aimed toward your becoming as persuasive as possible. Specifically, we will want to concentrate on communication techniques that help you achieve your call objectives when you are face to face with an important prospect. This means that how these business managers react to you becomes the important issue. In this regard, it is worthwhile to think about what their expectations are of you and why you must make an effort to perform accordingly.

These people tend to form conclusions and make lasting judgments on the fly. They don't let information stack up in their mind. Rather, they process data as it goes by and then they reduce it to conclusions, judgments, and opinions. This is one of their survival techniques; otherwise, they would be overdosed on information by week's end.

Let's focus on communication and associated skills in the context of a call situation. Picture yourself walking into your customer's office. You have done business with this account before, but you have never met with this particular gentleman. As you are shown into his office, you know that you are about to set the stage for your entire call.

The customer sees you and is immediately launching into the process of forming an impression of you. This same impression will also be applied later to your message. Only a minute has passed and, yet, the listener has labeled you and possibly everything that is to follow! (There is an old cliché: You never get a second chance to make a first impression! This is an absolute lie, but we'll deal with that later.)

Your communication has started. You are in the opening part of your call. Your customer is still giving you the twice over and surely your attire will pass this instant inspection. Your face and voice are now the focus of his attention. If this is a first meeting, you are likely to be shaking hands. Is this part of communicating? Think about it.

THE RIGHT TOUCH

Touching is one of the most intimate moments allowed in American business communications. Touching, in another context, is both personal and private. Lovers may hold hands and look deeply into each others eyes. Two old friends may shake hands using the double grasp approach, which shows the warmth of their greeting. In both cases, strong signals are being sent and received.

In our capacity as business people, we touch our hands to the hands of others every day. At the heart of this touching lies the opportunity to send signals to the other person. What kind of signals do you send?

The Handshake

Seldom, if ever, has anyone commented to you about your handshake, its qualities and the signals it sends. Why? Because touching is personal, and they wouldn't want to risk offending on a personal level. However, in the examination of communication nuances, we always want to ensure that the signals sent are the ones we want to send:

- I'm glad.
- I'm warm.
- I'm interested.
- I'm sincere.
- I'm honest.
- I'm comfortable with you.

Your prospect must recognize that a handshake is happening. Some people get in and out of a handshake so quickly you couldn't catch it with a high-speed shutter. How long is long enough? A little conscious practice will resolve this for you. Generally, you can continue the handshake through most of your initial greeting.

Your handshake should create a firm connection—you do want your signals to flow. The "limp" shake will pass no signal at all. Even worse, if one does get through, it can't be a positive one. Never use the double grasp handshake. This signals affection and isn't an acceptable business signal.

The touch is further conditioned by the tone of your voice—distinct, warm, and well modulated is the ticket. Speak slowly to maximize handshake time. You must look this listener in the eye. You will discover that the listener will most often glance away and then immediately return to your eyes—and you want to still be there. You haven't finished with all of your signals and the handshake is probably done with. You are still touching, but now you're doing it all with your eyes and your voice.

The Pleasant Expression

This isn't where you want to use your full-blown smile. It could be viewed as out of place. This is a business meeting, and your customer acts in certain ways when on the serious business side of the day. A "hint" of a smile will probably cause the pleasant expression you're looking for. But that expression doesn't end at your chin. It extends to include how your arms are held and the position of your body in relation to where the prospect is positioned. All of you should be "toward" the prospect.

Your friendly expression must be complemented by a voice that also sounds friendly and words that are equally friendly. The dimensions of these first few minutes must have matching characteristics. If one is flawed, then the others will lack the positive signals that you intended to send.

LINKAGE

Your sales call is constructed of spoken thoughts that build one upon the other. A series of these spoken thoughts is designed to describe a situation or achieve agreement on key points. Linkage is the process of getting from one of these key points to the beginning of the next one. What you say while linking depends on what was said and understood in the last subject. Linkage refers to the words and thoughts you use to move from where you are in your call to the next subject or plateau. Linkage not only connects, but it also does it in logical increments.

Connector words or connecting sentences alone do not provide linkage. These are used to help your explanation about a key thought flow logically. For example, during the call, you want to make the durability of your product a key issue. You plan to discuss four characteristics to support your point:

1. Statistical evaluations from an independent agency

2. Your company's maintenance experience

3. An example of the product's performance in stressful environments

4. Market acceptance and two customer testimonials

Connector words and connecting sentences are used to cause an easy and natural flow among the four points. You will conclude with a summary of how these points confirm product durability and how that translates into a benefit for those who purchase and use your product. You have now completed a key thought and are ready to move on to your next key thought. You will now use the linkage technique.

The linkage objective is to package the thought that you are leaving and to introduce your next thought. To achieve linkage, you have to build little bridges so that your audience can walk with you from one key thought to another. These little bridges are pieces of logic that carry you from one place to another. Additionally, they are testing points because you can check to see if your audience went across the bridge with you. Did the audience agree to your conclusions (the packaging) of the thought that you are now leaving? You may look back and see them still standing on the other end. It is vital that you discover whether the audience is crossing the bridge with you. While explaining your key thought (durability), you gave cause and actions as supporting evidence. The linkage is used to measure the effect and consequence of your effort.

Validation of Sales Call Progress

The idea of "cause and effect" can be helpful in testing whether linkage is logical and clear. Action/consequence is another useful testing technique. Both "cause" and "action" are more likely to reside in the body of your call. The "effect" and "consequence" parts become the first plateau of your bridges. They are the high octane ingredients that propel you forward. Your "feature/benefit" explanations are examples that you use in every call situation. These must be tightly linked to achieve the desired impact. If a benefit didn't have an effect, if it didn't have a consequence, then it also didn't have value.

At the upper management level, we can expect that our listener(s) has considerable experience in deductive reasoning and will quickly spot weak or marginal linkage. Such a listener may appear to let you get away with these soft linkages, but the odds are that you were quickly detected and your audience just quietly updated his or her mental score card. Therefore, using the feature/benefit example, you are advised to incorporate strong validation.

The validation step has real power. First, you get the customer involved. Therefore, a monologue has been promoted to a discussion. (This is where you want to be.) Next, the validation part lets you get a peek at that mental score card and gives you a chance to improve it. The validation part is an important slice of your bridge (the linkage structure) because you're asking your audience if they got across okay and if it is it all right to go on to the next major thought. If they didn't cross, you'll have to go back and lead them to the other side by expanding on and otherwise strengthening your logic sets. Remember that you can't push them over the bridge. If you try to push, and they appear (pretend) to go along, you're being fooled! You made them do it! Perhaps the only choice you gave them was to take exception and possibly appear rude, or to just appear to go along. What you get here may depend on which personality type you're dealing with. In any event, if they pretend now, they'll keep fooling you through the remainder of the call. In such a case, the call gets out of hand and you will likely begin to be a little confused. The reason is simply that you formed the wrong conclusion about your validation.

We've seen salespeople lose it all right here. There are two consequences worth looking at. First, you'll begin to lose control of the call, and, yes, to even become confused. You're thinking that they crossed over (successfully) and are on the same page as you. But they keep looping back, questioning something that you had already put in the bank. After several such misread validations, particularly where the audience is more than one person, no one, yourself included, has any idea just who is on what page. The whole call has become a mess!

The next consequence (caused by the first one) is that you have to attempt to recover or salvage something. Recovery is improbable, and a salvage operation must be invented on the fly. In either case, the price is that your original call objectives are down the tubes. Is everything lost? Perhaps not, but admit to yourself that you've taken some major hits and may be sinking fast. You may even find that your audience is beginning to enjoy this and if it is an audience group, the feeding frenzy is on! A graceful retreat may be your only option, and while there are several ways to pull this off, they fall outside our effective communication agenda.

Assumptive Linkage

Many salespeople also need linkage logic to get from a good opening into the body of the call. There may be very little to build on unless you have already made several calls within this account. If so, then information gathered on those calls can translate into a linkage statement on your next call. If not, we suggest that you use an "Assumptive Linkage." This requires greater courage (more moxie) but has only three parts:

1. Your stated assumption

2. The customer's response, which is likely to be a clarification, a correction, an adjustment, or flat-out rejection

3. Your updated assumption (and back to 2)

The idea here is to get your audience to help you build the linkage. Most often they are willing (eager) to help. For example:

You: Mr. Powell, The key items I have planned to discuss today are based on insights gained while working with some of my other customers. I found that their upper management had some concern about and real interest in the cost containment side of the PC explosion. Have you occasions to wonder what kinds of solutions are being developed to deal with this phenomenon? (WAIT)

Mr. Powell: We are aware that on an individual basis the cost seems small, but if lumped together, month after month, I suppose we would be surprised. Our people at the purchasing level are likely to be looking after that.

(Now is the time for a few probing questions, so that you can round out your revised assumption.)

You: Mr. Powell, several of my customers discovered that PC acquisition methods followed the same paperwork process as that used for much more expensive data processing equipment, and yet the volume was a hundred times larger. In their case, purchasing just staffed up to deal with the large transaction increases. Mr. Powell, I have found that this is also the approach being used in your company. I'm going to bet that you'd be interested in knowing about a better way. (WAIT to test your adjusted assumption.)

The basic linkage structure is beginning to take shape, but our sense is that Mr. Powell is still clinging to his earlier assumption that their purchasing group is "looking after that" because he doesn't want to get involved with how PCs are purchased. We can conclude that he is very close to suggesting that you could take your ideas to the purchasing people. You must prevent him from saying that.

On the other side of this linkage, you have a touchy story that you want to sell. You want Mr. Powell to understand that the purchasing folks fully intend to keep on doing things the old way. They may have little choice because they have little (if any) decision-making authority when it comes to adapting to a new acquisition approach, such as you have in mind. Additionally, you want to suggest that the end users of PCs are often frustrated in their attempts to satisfy their needs for PCs or upgraded components in a timely fashion. This causes productivity problems across a wide spectrum of his organization. The troops aren't happy!

As you can see, Mr. Powell didn't think that he was interested in PC acquisition methods, but he perks up considerably when confronted with productivity problems and even more when he learns that people are being unnecessarily frustrated. It is imperative that you have something real to back up your statements. For example, a newly hired planner had to borrow PC time for twenty-three work days although everything he needed was locally available within one working day! Mr. Powell will understand why you are in his office rather than downstairs talking to purchasing people. But let's press on to another dimension of your communications.

LISTENING AS AN ART FORM

Your customer is most comfortable, and feels in control, when he or she is talking. Your job at this time is to learn and then to immediately put the new information to work. It is difficult to not talk. It is also difficult to listen, particularly if you're thinking about what to say next and how to get back in control of the call. But it's okay for the customer to talk and to be in control. All you have to do is to provide them with a little guidance.

Interrupting the customer is acceptable because by "guidance" we mean helping the customer do a better job of talking about relevant issues. A "park it" interruption is a case in point. The customer has made a general or broad statement in which you see the potential for important details. You want those to surface and be remembered because you believe they may be important to your call objectives. Your "park it" interruption is designed to capture the broad statement and cause the customer to speak to the details. Phrases that lead into this type of interruption might be: "Excuse me, I find that to be an interesting point of view.

But does it also mean . . . and if so, would you always take the same course of action?"

If a customer can talk and can also be guided, it follows that he or she can also play a major role toward achieving your call objectives. So much the better, because customer-made points are retained longer than points that you make. A good way to think about guiding a call is to relate the process to signals that we all see while we are driving: Stop, Go, Turn Lane Only (left or right), Do Not Cross Over, Do Not Pass, Caution, and all the rest. Think about how these signals could be converted into words and how they can cause a change in direction:

Stop: I don't think that I understand that.

Go: Yes, I can understand that.

Turn: Then is it fair to say that you feel . . .

The ability to listen and learn can be validated by an amusing party game we invite you to play. At your next opportunity (a social gathering) select someone whom you do not know to be your playmate. The game rule is simply to find out all you can about this person without sharing anything about yourself. Do not share the rule with your selected playmate. Start with an opening statement immediately followed by your first question. You decide when the game is over. Never tell anyone that it was a game!

Isolating the Customer Isn't Smart

On the flip side of listening, we find the salesperson who just can't stop talking. This person feels there is some kind of code that says salespeople have an obligation to stay in control and to do all the talking. This person whips through the opening like a shrill winter's wind. Progress into the main body of the call (what the salesperson wants to talk about) is more like a quantum leap that is possible only because the customer is being bombarded with tons of words. Successive quantum leaps are used instead of linkage bridges. The audience isn't making these leaps and quickly gets left behind. They feign attentive listening but may already be moving toward disbelief or amazement. Our star, however, is following the code that says hearing is listening and listening is believing and staying in control is best done by continuous talking.

Customers or prospects very definitely react to all of the above. This isn't any fun for them but they can't seem to find a turnoff or kill switch. The next best option, however, is to tune out, and the technique is to stop listening; keep an attentive face, and then to just began thinking about something else. Anything will do. Mind wandering is next on this agenda and it takes only another small step to get there.

In the above example, the sales rep didn't learn anything, and neither did the customer. At "summary and close" time, the customer was in some other world. Fortunately, the sad events described above can have a happier side. Watching a seasoned professional salesperson at work in a call or presentation situation can be a fascinating experience. Below, the idea of listening as an art form is shown as the technique of moving and guiding the entire call.

Visualize the almost casual request for a response. The customer begins to speak, and the salesperson is glued to every word, listening intently as suggested by stillness and a slight inquisitive facial expression. A quiet moment occurs, and the salesperson inserts a gentle probe comment or question and the customer talks a little more. At the next quiet moment, the salesperson smoothly interjects a logical linkage statement and frames a relevant capability statement, ties it to a pertinent benefit, and then offers up the validation statement and then . . . sits quietly. The cycle is repeated, and with each repetition, an observer would notice that the salesperson is methodically progressing toward the call objective, and with the customer's concurrence.

"I'd like to make a note of that please." The sales pro described above probably used a yellow pad several times in the call. This technique is another form of gentle but firm probing. It always works! The customer will give you time to make your note. While making the note, there is time to speak another probe. The request to make the note was an acceptable interruption and even indicated that the customer said something important! Never leave with a blank yellow pad. That could be an insult. Some make notes but never ask for an interrupt. That's a waste of a very effective technique.

DESCRIPTIVE COMMUNICATIONS

Consider the real estate agent who shows the client an attractive four-bedroom, two-car garage home nestled in a pleasant neighborhood setting. Together they enter and begin to browse through the rooms, noting size, colors, and features. What an easy job. Very little descriptive detail is required because the client can see everything the agent sees. You may have experienced the following: The agent says, "Isn't this a large room?" This astute observation may be followed by, "You can see that the kitchen has all the necessary appliances." In fairness we should admit that it's tough to find words to describe something that is equally obvious to both parties.

However, consider the builder who takes a client to a plot of land located on a peaceful knoll just minutes away from easy access to the city. As they stand and thoughtfully look at the site, nothing happens until the client begins to slowly visualize the growth of a charming home. The builder should help this visualization with situational descriptive communications: a word-picture home, with a word-picture family, enjoying word-picture benefits. The builder's challenge requires more skill than was necessary for the real estate agent. Even so, the client has seen many homes and even lives in a home now. The builder's word pictures relate to a visualization of expectations that the client can easily accept.

The salesperson has a much greater challenge than that of the builder of fine homes. It seems to us that you must create descriptive situations about events that may or may not occur, place your prospect into those situations, describe the probable impact of being in those situations, and extrapolate into a value-added attribute in such a way that the prospect feels it is important! How does this relate to us?

Remember, again, all that we are saying assumes that you are into an Account Development process and that your calls are on upper management types. These people are often called "big picture types" because they have to perceive the value added from your description of your overall capabilities. Therefore you have to paint the picture so that the "big picture types" see all the colors (benefits), marvel at the delicate brush strokes (communication skills), and buy into the finished canvas. Consequently, the following section is intended to help you recognize and fine-tune your word picture skills.

The Power of Word Pictures

Your story is your canvas.

Benefits are your colors.

Techniques become your brush strokes.

And, as always, the customer is the critic.

A word alone seldom carries a message. It is how a person groups words together, or strings them, that causes information to be transferred. Words make thoughts, thoughts make sentences, and it takes multiple sentences to form the spoken paragraph that holds your word picture. So your paragraph has to be substantive enough for your customer to get the picture. Look at other words whose meanings also can convey this idea of a picture: illustration, depiction, representation, envision, facsimile, imagine. All of these words should describe what you want to do.

If what you say doesn't seem to complete the picture, it might be that you are assuming that your audience is listening to what you are saying and reading your mind simultaneously. Isn't it better to tread lightly on the mind reading part so as to increase the chances that they can arrive at the same picture that you intended to paint? You can't depend on them to be aware of things you did not say.

For example, suppose we are calling on our Mr. Powell, the executive. We have met resistance to change at lower levels and we want to convey this to Mr. Powell and cause him to be motivated to intervene. In this example, our word picture needs to include the following thoughts:

- Old ways may not be best ways.

- Alternatives are available.

- My company has the best track record.

- I want a chance.

First let's net out what we want to get across. We want to suggest that people repetitively do things the same old way even when it is no longer the best way. Next, we want him to agree that they should look at new ways. Our product has been redesigned, has new characteristics, and deserves to be considered. This is the focus of our word picture. We want to imply that his people (subordinates) are too comfortable to even look at what we have. We want him to zap their comfort zone. We want to be tactful, yet get it all said:

"Mr. Powell, when people are practiced at something, then they are probably good at it and it seems to make sense to continue doing it that way. It can be both easy and safe. Even so, Mr. Powell, that would also imply that other things were also remaining the same, which as we both know, is probably not so. Recognizing this, my company reviewed our design criteria for this product, knowing that our customers would be looking to us to provide new answers for new problems as well new answers for old problems."

We hope you know that we were building a picture of "old ways may not be best ways!" Read our words again, then look away and create a validation statement. Validate that Mr. Powell heard, understood, and accepted what was said. Do it now.

Several validation statements could get the job done. In any of them, you're attempting to find out if Mr. Powell got the picture (saw it) and agreed to it. Did he buy into the idea that old ways are not necessarily the best ways? If so, you can now validate that he will look at a new way. So we have named two things that you want to validate.

Here is one of *our* validation statements: "Mr. Powell, I suppose you frequently come across procedures that need to be updated and even changed; is that true?" (Powell responds yes). "Do you find that for some people, the old way is guarded as the best way, and it is hard to convince them to change?" (Powell admits that this, too, is true.) In the face of all this, Mr. Powell, do you feel that there is a way that our newly designed product could get a receptive audience in your company; and, if so, can you suggest how I could go about making that happen?"

If our validation statements (and questions) work the way that we intended, Mr. Powell agrees that new ways often merit consideration and might be implemented to replace the old way. He admits that everyone is not so receptive to such change. He will suggest how to get our newly designed product in front of the right people. He is about to become our sponsor! Mr. Powell is also likely to add that he doesn't make those kinds of product decisions, but we knew this all along. We also know how to make this conversation have impact as we continue our Account Development activities.

Before going on, we should tie up one loose end. Earlier in this chapter, we said you can get a second shot at making a first impression. Most people are willing to change a previous impression. In the examples here, the salesperson became a good listener. He or she developed logical linkages and painted word pictures, all of which made a positive impression on Mr. Powell. When done well, these will overshadow that very first impression. Most would agree that we can build on successes, but the reality is that we can also build on a failure. How could we sell day after day if we didn't believe that!

MAINTAINING A POSITIVE ATTITUDE

Calls on upper-level people are too important to risk blowing. The appointment may have been difficult to get. Your attitude about this call is worth thinking about. This call is a business meeting between two business people. Do you think of yourself that way? We hope you don't feel the executive is doing you a favor. We hope you feel there is a good reason for your being there. There is something worthwhile you can do for this person as well as for this company.

We know you aren't going to make a sale during this call, at least not in the normal sense of making a sale. However, you have objectives for the call, and if you achieve them, you can score that as a sale!

All we have said in this chapter can be affected by your attitude as you begin to make your call. If you feel like "Wow, what an opportunity; and I can't wait to get it on," chances are that you are truly ready and close to your peak. You're feeling good about yourself and what can be accomplished. You're probably supported in this regard by knowing that you've done your homework and that this is going to be a professional sales call.

If you haven't prepared well and aren't charged up, you have turned the call over to those villains named "fate" and "chance," and you may be concerned about how well this call is going to go. How effective can your communications be when you feel this way? Why did you let this happen to you?

Equally fatal is an attitude that can attack people who sell more often than those in any other profession. During a sales call, have you ever felt as though you were begging, that you wanted something (your objectives) too much? It happens to all of us sometimes. But we should be on the lookout for this feeling because there is no way that it can help you sell. If you convey this feeling in some way to your prospect, the most you can expect is that he or she will feel sorry for you. Their sympathy will last only for a moment, however, and can never be converted into a reason to buy.

If you sense that you're begging, step back and think through what is going on with you. Say to yourself, "Hold everything. What is happening to cause this feeling?" We suspect that in the past, you have reviewed several dimensions of your job and were pleased with your evaluation. Nothing has changed:

1. You know your product is good and, while it doesn't meet the current needs of everyone, others have used it countless times, it stands on its own merits. So you don't have to "beg" on behalf of your product.

2. If your prospect ends up buying your product, he or she is going to experience certain benefits. You can describe these benefits and back them up with logic as well as with relevant references and/or testimonials of others who did buy and benefit.

3. Your price is competitive and very fair. It is not a complicated pricing structure, and there are no tricks involved. You wouldn't sell it if this were not so.

4. You want to make this sale, but the world won't end if you don't. You have many choices, such as the following:

   ◆ If rejected, you can call it a day and start fresh tomorrow

   ◆ There are other prospects, some of whom will buy.

   ◆ You can go on welfare.

Salespeople have to ask for things. Prospects and customers expect that. Easy examples are, "Will you sign the order today?," "Will you introduce me to the manager of that group?," "Will you read my proposal?," "Would you arrange for me to meet with the committee?" In each example, it is assumed that the salesperson has conveyed the logic (the sales foundation) to justify asking the question. This isn't begging. It is selling!

So on reflection, it's almost silly to feel like you are begging. Even so, it's necessary to move beyond this feeling to others that are more positive. The best way known is to STOP, THINK, RESOLVE, and then push on with a determined spurt of new activity with other prospects. You will certainly have to repeat this process on another day, but you will overcome the negative feelings each time and in the same way. It's the old philosophy of saying that regardless, you're gonna drive one more nail, and then another, and then another! One of those next nails is going to drive home, true and certain. That is a sale made, and it won't happen because you were begging! It'll happen because you're selling and because you just "keep on keeping on." So when, and if, this attitude crops up, go through the logic above and sink it 16 fathoms deep!

SCOTT'S SOLUTION

The negative perception described in Scott's dilemma is one of the toughest we have ever encountered. Many businesses, including some of Scott's accounts, have had to also deal with their own negative deeds and resulting publicity. Today, such exposure is at an all-time high and includes such things as environmental waste disposal, unfriendly takeovers, issuance of junk bonds, foreign labor, illegal practices, plant shutdowns, discrimination suits, and so on. Even so, most of these may leave only a negative taste that "it's a bad company." In the case of Seaboard Metals, the question is about survival and ownership. This tends to be much more serious in the minds of companies that depend on Seaboard as a supplier.

Scott has the difficult task of shoring up the business relationship between Seaboard and its customers. In this regard, he must put together a convincing story, which concludes that Seaboard isn't going to go away. This story must include financial realities coupled with some description of management's recovery plans.

Next, Scott must plan to make a series of "one-on-one" presentations of this material to all of his key contacts in all accounts that are important to him. He is well-advised to make executive calls also because it is at these levels that sudden decisions can be made based on their certain knowledge of what has been printed about Seaboard.

Meeting with an executive, with the objective of dispelling or neutralizing negative perceptions, is about as tough as a selling situation can get. In addition to a convincing story, Scott will need to use all of the power communication techniques discussed in this chapter.

We would suggest that Scott quickly visit buyer and user contacts. He should follow with visits on the key financial and manufacturing executives. Good opening lines can evolve from a theme that says, "I'm here to thank you for the business you've given to my company and to also tell you about some things going on at Seaboard and what we're doing about them." The call objective is to put negative perceptions into a nonthreatening perspective and to earn the right to ask the customer to stick with us. The way in which this is communicated can make all the difference.

■■■■■■■■■■■■

CHAPTER 6

CALLING HIGH

A Tough Selling Situation:

Entrenched Competition
and Resistance to Change

You're out and they're in. The customer's users and buyers aren't going to rock a boat that's drifting along okay. Their job is to keep things moving with what they have. Your competitor knows this and depends on their entrenched status and the customer's resistance to change something that's working all right. If you want "in," you're face-to-face with a very tough selling situation.

KEVIN

Kevin Fulton was spending Friday afternoon reviewing the week's events. He sold a line of high performance copy machines and every qualified prospect was important. Kevin kept a good account control book, and it was his habit to update it every week. His largest prospect was McClain Industries, but he had been unable to make any conclusive progress there. They were one of the country's largest manufacturers of small to medium gasoline engines incorporating leading edge technology developed by their acclaimed engineering department.

Kevin had spoken to the purchasing agent at McClain's Milwaukee plant. He was told that everyone seemed happy with their currently installed copiers and that procurements would probably be about the same as in the past. Kevin had talked by phone with two contacts at McClain's plant in Bridgeport and got the same story. If history repeats, Kevin knew that his competitor would automatically get 6 to 10 new orders for upgrades or replacements this year and would end up with about 35 large copy machines throughout McClain's facilities.

Kevin's company had just introduced a new line of copiers (8000 Series) designed for centralized "duplication centers." The 8000 included optional remote microfiche readers that could input engineering drawings over a local area network. The 8000 could also report job status to LAN connected PCs. The implications were awesome.

The greatest insight came when Kevin thought through the product and sales strategy developed and espoused by his company. The 8000 Series was specifically targeted to the high end of the reproduction market. The new lines also dictated that customers buy into the idea of centralized copy/reproduction centers. Associated expenditures were significant; the dollar justification had to be related to new functions and the integration of networks, microfiche, and remote PCs.

Kevin would need to convince customers that they should organize their copy/reproduction processes in such a fashion that they could take advantage of the most current technology and the resulting benefits. In the case of McClain, this would mean that someone there would have to embrace the idea of major change. Who at McClain could cause a rethinking of their approach to the whole reproduction process? Why would he or she do this? Kevin's assessment of his situation at McClain Industries was becoming much more focused. He needed to shuffle the deck and deal himself a new hand!

How "high" is high enough? To get into the right range, you must understand the size, scope, and operational characteristics of your customer and couple this with what it is you're trying to make happen. The Account Development process discussed in Chapter 2 established the broad objectives, and calling high is about the only way to really develop any account. Accept the reality that you need to move further up the ladder to find sponsorship and endorsement. If you can't or won't do this, then you're just another peddler on the block.

Much like other selling skills, calling high takes practice and opportunity for refinement. You must be swinging the bat if you ever intend to start making solid hits. Calling high isn't so hard to do; it's just difficult to get started. As a colleague of ours once said, "You don't have to call high on all your accounts; just the ones you want to keep." Calling high, and learning to comfortably do it well, makes you feel good! It adds an exciting dimension to the hard job of selling.

Why You Should Consider Calling High

New accounts and improved penetration of established accounts are your sources of stable growth. In today's highly competitive selling environment, you need every edge you can get just to stay in place, let alone to grow. That's why you should call high if you're not already doing so, and improve your executive selling skills if you are.

Your objective is maximum exposure. Calling high is selling your company and its capabilities to the chief operating executive of the area to which you target your services or products. Your objective is to gain maximum exposure within the prospect's organization by earning the endorsement of one or more key executives. This will lead to sponsorship for your proposal at the upper management level plus the next echelon down; and, ultimately, to cooperation from the company's buyers and users.

Launching your drive from the top has several advantages:

1. It helps you identify the maximum number of needs that can be matched to your products or services because the executive sees the forest, not just the trees. That gives you the opportunity to offer the broadest possible range of solutions when you later call on the decision makers who buy or directly influence the actual purchasing.

2. You set the stage to move down effectively to those decision makers because the executives whose attention and endorsement you've gained will direct you to them. Understand that when an executive gets interested in something, he or she will likely immediately delegate all or part of the work load. Also, he or she will also loop back later to inspect the progress made.

3. You leave your competition behind. It is unlikely that your competitors are calling at the executive level. The truth is that most salespeople just don't call very high. It takes work to be a professional!

When to Call High

Calling high is a time-consuming process. Thus, it is an appropriate strategy only for key accounts or those with the potential to grow to that status. Moreover, it is most appropriate when the services or products you are selling represent a major expenditure for the customer or involve significant productivity issues. The point is that if your assessment is that the account is unlikely to grow significantly no matter what you do, then don't waste your time. The exception is that if your revenue is already consequential, then protect it with a measured Account Development effort.

Bear in mind that executives think in terms of the next year and on, while the buyers you usually call on probably think in terms of the next six months or perhaps only "what's next." If all you have to talk about are minor matters, stick to calling on the buyer. Calling too high, without a good story to tell, is as big a mistake as the practice of always calling low.

Six sales situations are ideal candidates for executive sales calls:

1. *The New Account with Big Potential.* The perfect time to make an executive call is at the beginning of your sales effort. By starting at the top, you can develop a workable understanding of the organization's goals, plans, and problems. Once you have this knowledge of your prospect's situation, your chance of linking your product or service to its strategies gets better every day.

   To take advantage of this approach, you must be able to present your company and its capabilities so that the executive learns enough to be able to refer you to the appropriate decision makers—those who are directly involved in operations that can benefit from your capabilities. These executive referrals will open doors for you that might otherwise be closed or go undiscovered. Most other sales approaches won't do that for you.

2. *The Account Not Fully Tapped.* As an established supplier, you provide a valuable service or product to your customer. You know that other parts of the customer's organization could make use of your capabilities. It is usually difficult to locate these additional sales opportunities, however, because your current buyers are un-

likely to have more than a limited understanding of their entire organization. Also, political rivalries, organizational competition, and budget issues can make it awkward for users to give you internal referrals. Even if they did, such referrals would probably be horizontal rather than upward.

Your customer's executives and upper-level managers don't have such limitations and will also have a different viewpoint. These people are responsible for the success of entire operations. They are interested in seeing that effective answers are made available wherever possible. They can also get somewhat intrigued with new information and/or new ideas and may be constantly asking themselves how they can apply it.

When you can show to senior managers that you can help them reach their financial and productivity goals, they will be willing to provide you with new contacts. Your successful track record in their company should enable you to make an effective presentation.

Let your current contacts know of your plans to call on executives. Point out that you want everyone in their organization to be aware of what is being accomplished by your company. Be sure, too, that they understand that you will discuss any outcome with them as soon as possible. By approaching senior management when everything is going smoothly, you are less likely to ruffle your contacts' feathers. Still, they will sometimes try to discourage you from going over their heads, perhaps due to fear of what you might reveal to top management. To mitigate hard feelings, tell them your manager insists that you make the call. If an account warrants the Account Development effort, "I'll try," isn't good enough. Calling high has to happen.

Selling directly to a customer's buyers, or "traditional selling," puts you into a head-on contest with your competitors. This is the war zone, and you don't have leverage or any advantage. This is also the "react" zone because that is about all you can do. Not many new things are (or can be) considered in the war zone, because their soldiers are merely carrying out orders . . . or what they perceive to be their orders. These soldiers get very careful when they have to choose the supplier. They don't want to make subjective decisions because these are difficult to defend at some later date if a challenge is raised. They also want to be very fair or to appear as though they were. You don't want them to be fair; you want them to be biased toward you, your product, and your company. How are you going to make that happen?

Calling on executives, or "top-down selling," gives you an edge over your competitors. While they continue to call on the end users, you earn door-opening endorsements from the top, get a fuller picture of the customer's general needs, and earn references to users you may not even have known about. You can bring down subtle thoughts and messages from above that might persuade users and buyers to change or modify their priorities. The premise is that you can help them to better achieve larger objectives. They can even become more fair, but more fair to their company. In this regard, they can reject suppliers who don't understand the larger objectives or somehow don't meet these subjective product requirements.

Be wary when your current contacts attempt to prevent you from calling at a higher level. Quite possibly, they are concealing some very important concerns. For example, there might be significant budget changes underway, intentions or negotiations for reorganization, or even plans to switch to a competitor. In such situations, it is especially important for you to establish executive contacts. You have to find out what is going on so that you will have time to plan and react. Also, asking a buyer or other lower contact to carry "your ball" to higher management levels for understanding or consideration is risky at best and should be avoided. If in fact they can do this, be aware that your message is going to become buried within their own agenda and will carry their initials. Therefore, you will have to become the work pawn of someone who doesn't make key decisions and can't sponsor you or your company.

3. *The Account That Needs Protection.* The case for an executive sales approach in this situation can be made on one point alone: If your business is not protected on the executive level, you are always vulnerable to a high-level attack by your competitors. Your best accounts are your competitors' most tempting targets. If those competitors come in at the top before you've told your story there, they may displace you.

Also remember that most organizations scrutinize expenditures regularly. During times when money is tight or when business is slow, even small expenditures may have to be justified (all over again). You can't assume that your buyer's boss is telling your company's story at the next level up. And if he or she is not, it is possible that your base is not adequately protected from predatory competitors.

Rather than relying on the possibility that someone is doing your selling for you, be sure to cover your own bases by establishing executive relationships. Establishing relationships with key executives also gives you a valuable source of help when you are having problems at lower levels. If you have told your story during good times, you will have credibility when things aren't going so well.

The worst time to introduce yourself on the executive floor is when you are the bearer of bad tidings. Still, it may sometimes be the right course. If bad news travels upstairs without your side of the story, your situation could become even more troubling. In fact, you could lose the business.

4. *The Competitive Diversion.* Calling at the top can be an extremely useful diversionary tactic when you are trying to counter a competitor's attack. Suppose that you are in a nip-and-tuck competition with a competitor for a new account. You may well gain an advantage by confusing your competitor's efforts and priorities.

Find out which account is your competitor's biggest local customer. Make courtesy calls on its key executives, and leave your brochures, catalogs, and sales literature around the building. It won't be long before your competitor learns that you have been calling on its "cash cow." Its sales rep will immediately backtrack to protect the account, leaving the prospect to you for the time being.

A personal account of one such situation may help to illustrate this tactic. The prospect was a large manufacturer of over-the-road semi-trailers, and the primary contact was the vice president of manufacturing. The in-place competitor was in solid. The prospect was never sold, but good rapport was developed with the vice president. Brief calls were made on him frequently, enlightening him with a new story, a new slant, or a new capability in the world of manufacturing control systems. He was encouraged to look at what his supplier had or did not have in this area. He caught onto the game and kept his supplier constantly off balance. He was given an edge and he used it to the hilt. The hints usually took only minutes to devise, but the competitor sometimes spent days in preparing responses, complete with management visits and flights to demonstrations at other customer sites. These actions were so deliberate and so much fun—a ticking bomb was left on each visit . . . and the competitor had to defuse every one!

5. *The Best and Final Effort.* In almost any sales territory, you will find a few dinosaurs. Dinosaurs are huge accounts that might well be extinct because, for whatever reason, you simply haven't been able to get their business. Typically, you have spent much time and effort responding to bids, analyzing requirements, and submitting proposals. Possibly, you have reached the limit of your patience and are willing to write off the account.

If you are convinced, however, that you deserve the account, and it is potentially big enough to warrant one final effort, then present your case as high up as possible. Since the user and/or buyer level is producing nothing for you, you really have nothing to lose by going right to the top.

These are excellent accounts to approach first if you are hesitant about calling high. There is little risk involved because your management has no expectations for them. If your efforts are successful, you have everything to gain.

Your activities in these cases, particularly if you are successful, will probably make some people at the customer's lower levels unhappy. After all, they have probably been the ones blocking you out. When you shake up these people in this manner, they may try to shun you and certainly will not promote your cause in their company. Be prepared to document your progress and keep your executive contact informed when it is appropriate.

6. *The Executive-Level Protest.* This is the most urgent situation and the one in which you are least likely to succeed. Most experienced salespeople have lost business when they know they should have won it. Buyers sometimes use questionable judgment or make costly mistakes in choosing a supplier. When you are sure that you should have won, but someone less qualified got the order, you may wish to lodge a protest at the executive level. Some large, formal procurements include a set procedure for lodging a protest. When one is available, play it by the rules. However, most organizations have no provision for formal challenges to their buying decisions. When this is the case, you may proceed on your own.

Act quickly to identify the key operations executive, document your case, and get a hearing. You are asking the executive to reverse someone else's decision, so be prepared with very powerful and logical arguments. You won't have any trouble getting the appointment to state your case. Just tell the executive secretary that you wish to see this company officer to discuss a procurement practice that prohibits fair competition in his company. You'll get the appointment, but you are also walking on thin ice!

Be sure to involve your management in the process. Protest actions are typically messy and controversial. Caution and diplomacy are your watchwords here. But remember, lodging an executive level protest puts you in a situation where you have little or nothing to lose and much to gain. If you lose, don't bother coming back. On the other hand, if you already had a good Account Development plan established in the account, you would have never had to endure "the best and final effort" or the "protest" scenario.

A PLAN FOR SUCCESS

Let's examine what is involved in making sales calls on executives. Experience has shown that successful executive sales programs are the result of a cooperative effort. Where possible, sales and sales management work together to carry out the executive selling strategy. Ideally, the role of each person is clearly defined from the beginning.

You are responsible for the following activities:

- Researching the possible targets.

- Selecting the accounts to be pursued, in consultation with your manager.

- Building up a thorough business management structure file on the targeted organizations to include annual reports, news articles, financial reports, a description of major business activities, problems, goals, organization charts, and biographies of key people (anything you can get your hands on).

- Developing an executive selling plan and going over it with your manager. It is important that your manager buy into and become a co-owner of your plan.

After you have done your preparation for an executive sales call, you have to secure the appointment. Before phoning the executive's office, however, take the following steps:

- Find out the appropriate executive's name, title, and span of control. Whoever answers the phone for the company probably can give you this information. Public relations and personnel offices, as well as stories in the press and the annual reports and securities filings of publicly held companies, are also helpful.

- Find out the name of the executive's secretary from the company's phone operator.

- Pick a theme for the meeting. Be sure that it suits both your aim and the executive's expertise and responsibilities.

- Select alternate times and dates for the appointment. Allow two to three weeks lead time to improve the odds that the executive's schedule won't be fully booked.

- Develop a Tele-Chart for yourself (see Figure 6.1).

- Decide which executive you will call next if your first choice is unavailable and fails to recommend someone else.

If your target company is publicly held, consider buying its stock. As a stockholder, you'll have access to a broad range of information. You'll also enhance your credibility with the account.

TELE-CHART TO THE APPOINTMENT

One of the toughest parts of the Account Development process is getting a definite appointment with the people you've selected in upper management. This requires a plan, good techniques, diligence, patience, and perseverance. In many, if not most cases, they aren't used to seeing someone like you appear on their calendar. Most of the people they schedule time with are internal people. They are tracking programs and activities already underway, particularly those

Figure 6.1— Tele-Chart

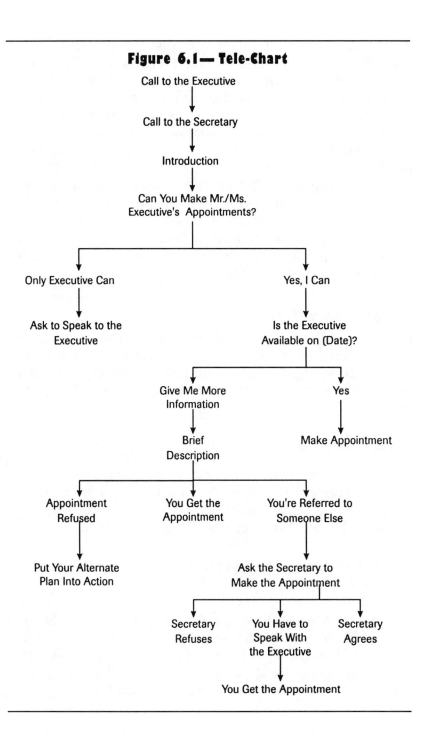

where they have a guiding role to play. So you have to cut through their routine and become an exception. They don't really want exceptions. Their office procedures and daily routines are carefully guarded over by the executive secretary. She is a formidable hurdle, and it will require both tactics and finesse to get her approval and help.

Following is a tested approach for securing an appointment with an executive via the telephone. It is not intended to be used verbatim. The words should be your own. Note the differences in approach between the conversation with the executive's secretary and the one with the executive. To whomever you speak, remember that you are not trying to sell on the phone. You are simply trying to obtain an appointment with the executive.

The Secretary Gateway

Below is a suggested phone conversation model with an executive secretary. It will give you an idea about how such a conversation might develop and lead to where you want to be. When the secretary answers, the call should flow as follows:

Secretary: [Mr./Ms. Executive's] office.

You: Hello, is this [Secretary's Name]? My name is [. . .], and I represent [Name of Your Company]. I am calling to make an appointment with [Mr./Ms. Executive]. Do you make [Mr./Ms. Executive's] appointments?

If the answer is yes, the secretary will want additional information:

You: I am with [Name of Your Company]. I want to talk to [Mr./Ms. Executive] to discuss [state the chosen theme of your call] at [name of prospect's company]. Is [Mr./Ms. Executive's] calendar open for 20 minutes on [date] in the morning, or is the afternoon better?

Note the repetition of your company's name. This is intentional. It helps the secretary track whom you represent without having to ask you to repeat yourself.

If the secretary requests more information, do the following:

- Avoid giving details beyond your theme.

- Repeat the request for a 20-minute appointment.

- Ask again what day and time is convenient.

- Do your best to avoid being shunted to a subordinate.

- Emphasize that you know the executive has responsibility for [. . .] and would be interested in talking with you.

If the answer is no, the secretary does not make appointments—or is unwilling to grant you an appointment—ask to speak with the executive directly.

If the secretary asks for your number, here are some possible actions:

- Be persistent. Repeat your theme and the reasons you believe the executive will wish to meet with you.

- Ask when your call will be returned.

- Ask if you can call back when the executive will be in the office.

If you leave a message and your phone call is not returned, call back. Why not? We can attest to the fact that the executive floor needs input from the outside world! Figure 6.1 diagrams the procedure of making an appointment with the executive through the executive secretary.

Direct Contact with the Executive

Some executives answer their own phones. Be prepared for this possibility. They won't be expecting you because almost all of their calls come from within their own organization.

Therefore the probability is that you have just surprised them and they are momentarily a tad off balance. Take this into consideration and let them catch up.

When you reach Mr./Ms. Executive, you'll want to try this approach:

> **You:** [Mr./Ms. Executive], my name is [. . .]. I represent [Name of Your Company]. I'm calling to arrange a 20-minute meeting with you to discuss how companies like [name of prospect's company] can [state a benefit]. I will need only about 20 minutes. Would [day and time] be convenient? Or would [day and time] be better for you?

Anticipate two principal objections when asking for an executive appointment. Prepare your answers in advance and you will increase your chance of getting the meeting.

Objection 1: Delegation. This is an attempt to refer you to someone else in the company. While this does fall within the objection category, remember that you are messing up someone's routine. The person on the other end of the phone is thinking "why me?" The easiest course of action is to get you to agree that seeing someone else is what you should really be doing. This is entirely normal, so you should expect it most of the time. Be ready.

> **Executive:** Perhaps you should talk with my vice president in charge of [. . .].

> **You:** [Mr./Ms. Executive], I would be happy to discuss this with your vice president. However, [explain why you wish to see this particular executive]. Is a morning or afternoon appointment better for you?

Objection 2: No Time. This may really mean no time to see sales representatives. If you didn't buy into the delegation maneuver, then by definition, you have invited this objection. Therefore, it is usually inevitable and you should expect it. It's part of the game, and both of you have to go through with the play. A dominant personality type might put you to a real test here by saying "No, I won't see you." You'll get no respect unless you reply, "Why not?"

Executive: I just don't have the time to talk with you.

You: [Mr./Ms. Executive], I know the demand on your time is great, and I know the time you spend with someone is an investment that must yield a return to your organization. The 20 minutes you invest with me will, I strongly believe, prove valuable to you. We will discuss the benefits of [state your theme] and how other companies have enhanced this area of their business. Could we meet [day and time] or would [day and time] be more convenient?

Sales reps who regularly pursue executive calls say that they get appointments better than 50 percent of the time using these approaches. However, if the executive still refuses to meet with you and directs you to a subordinate, leave the door open by doing the following:

- Agree to see the subordinate.

- Ask if the executive or his or her secretary would arrange the meeting.

- If neither will arrange the meeting, ask if the executive or the secretary will inform the subordinate that you will be calling.

- Request to get in touch with the executive after you meet with the subordinate.

- Ask the executive to attend any presentation you may plan to give at his or her company. His or her promised attendance will give you leverage with other company executives.

Your primary goal is to get an interview with the company's most senior relevant executive. However, if you are unable to do so, do not think that your call has failed. Strive to gain the executive's endorsement for a call on another executive. That endorsement will be worth the call. So if you "lose," you can still win. How does it feel to lose 50 percent of the time? We hope that you can say, "It feels great because my glass is half full all the time!"

Executives who won't meet with you will usually direct you to someone else without your asking. If they don't, ask them to do so. And don't be concerned that the person will have too little influence. It is unlikely that a top executive will refer you to someone who is not a peer or associate. Ask, "Could you direct me to someone else who is involved in this area?" Our estimate is that you have a better than 75 percent chance of getting the appointment with the referred executive or manager because of the higher executive's suggestion.

On the other hand, if you've done your homework, there is a tactic that can allow you to loop back and go for this appointment again. You can suggest that the reason for selecting him or her was not an accident. For example, you might say, "The things I need to talk about will require someone with a strong background in engineering design techniques, and I know about your training and experience in that area." You've stated a fact; you've fed an ego, and you've cut the options for an escape path. Now this is not a deception. It's just good, clean, hard selling.

Keep It Simple

Be aware that your presentation should be organized around a single theme, for example, savings through the use of refurbished computer systems, or cost containment through just-in-time (JIT) decision tools. The theme should be simple enough to be communicated on the phone when you are asking for an appointment. If you can't state your theme in 10 words or less, you need to rethink it, simplify it, and make it more pointed.

When you make the actual call, your conversation should remain at a broad, conceptual level and refer repeatedly to the chosen theme. Once you slip from the conceptual to the specific, you may lose the executive's interest and be directed to a lower-level company official. You do not want that to happen at this point. What you are after now is an endorsement that will open doors for you and referrals that will tell you whose doors to approach. You also want to establish a relationship between the account's top management and your organization. Sometime in the future, it is these same relations that might help to protect your business in this account. Tie this thought back to the fact that an Account Development effort is one that is constantly building toward future events and opportunities. In this regard, bricks laid weeks and months earlier give you a safe and firm place to stand on today, while protecting your business in the future.

Eight Steps to Prepare for the Call

Before meeting with an executive, take the following preparatory steps:

1. Request biographical information about the executive from his or her secretary. This will give you a better idea of the executive's areas of expertise. It may also reveal social, educational, or philanthropic connections that you share with the executive. These can help you build a relationship.

2. Send a letter confirming your appointment and restating the meeting's theme. Include your biography.

3. Review the company profile, which you should have in your "Key Account" dossier.

4. Prepare general information on your company, including several success stories.

5. Review the recommended timed outline and write your presentation. Incorporate appropriate information about your company.

6. Pre-plan the activities that will follow the executive appointment. Define your goals specifically. You want to be prepared to move when the executive suggests other names to call on within his or her organization.

7. Rehearse your presentation. Be sure it does not exceed 20 minutes.

8. Select alternative sales activities that you can put into action if the meeting does not turn out as you expected. For example, try to meet with another executive, schedule a demonstration, or hold a sales seminar.

Executives' schedules are usually planned in 15- or 30-minute segments. By asking for 20 minutes, you automatically give the executive the option of expanding your visit by half without altering his or her other plans for the day. Moreover, when you ask for 20 minutes, you sound like a concise, time-conscious professional who knows what he or she is doing. When thinking about your timing, consider that 10 minutes belong to you, and the other 10 minutes belongs to the other person. (Don't be concerned if you have little experience yet. Executives often go out of their way to help younger representatives, especially if they have a son or daughter about the same age).

THE EXECUTIVE SALES CALL

The three distinct parts of an executive call, building rapport and opening, discussion, and closing, serve an important function. Here is a breakdown of each, along with a suggested dialogue to get you started. As with the Tele-Chart dialogue, use our ideas but use your own words.

Build Rapport/Open

The sales representative opens the appointment and then proceeds to state the purpose of the meeting:

Thank you, [Mr./Ms. Executive], for this opportunity to sit and talk with you about [theme of meeting—expand as needed]. My company has recently upgraded our dispatching and routing capabilities, which can offer our customers attractive shipping alternatives. We've always been very competitive but believe that now we are stepping out with some unique strengths. The planned purpose of our meeting today is to find out if your corporate objectives can be helped by these strengths. To provide a framework for our discussion, I would like to take a few minutes to provide you with a perspective on how I think your company might assess our capabilities.

Discussion

There are three parts to the discussion: a lead-in, the presentation itself, and the executive's response. The discussion at large should describe your company's achievements in the business, illustrating them with a few examples. Success stories are best, but never reference a competitor of the executive's company. Here is a recommended presentation, which is intended to be put into your own words:

Your opening and lead-in:

[Mr./Ms. Executive], [Name of Your Company] is a principal contributor in the field of [industry/product]. We've built our success by helping our customers save money, save time, and become more effective in moving product out. Our aim is to help our customers manage their resources and meet their business objectives.

Presentation:

The next step is to develop a commentary on your company's investments in or commitment to your field.

To illustrate this: [work up examples, mentioning your achievements in other customer organizations that relate to the prospect's needs as you perceive them. Use relevant examples. Include appropriate "war stories" and cite major industry results, without naming specific customers].

Executive's Response:

The executive will probably respond as soon as you finish. If not, it is up to you to elicit a response by asking a leading question. The following, for example, would be at the end of the presentation and clearly gives the floor to the executive.

Representative: *To better understand how we can benefit your organization, would you share with us the direction in which your company is heading in this regard and your thoughts about the information I have just presented?*

Base your question on your observation of the executive's reactions during the discussion. The above suggestion may sound a bit formal, but it's okay to sound this way because it shows respect. In any event, you want to find out what the executive thinks of your idea and what you are offering his or her organization. Be prepared to respond to any of the following:

- Current thoughts associated with your discussion topic. For example, if your theme was data processing cost management, the executive might respond by commenting on EDP budgets, controls, and so forth. If you represented a shipper, you might expect a response relating to their tight schedules and the commitments they make to their customers. You can expect the response to be relevant.

- *What's just been said about your organization.* Here, the executive might ask for details about the results you achieved at another company, or what kinds of problems were encountered.

- *Current concerns about your discussion topic and its applicability to his or her organization.* The executive may not be sure that your solution is applicable given the current environment in his or her company. Or, budgets may be a problem.

- *How you could help his or her organization.* The executive is asking you to expand your comments on how you can apply your capabilities to the needs of his or her company. He or she may feel the need to refer you to people who have a more detailed understanding of those requirements.

- *"How can we go on?" "What's next?"* The executive may want more information or may wish to schedule a follow-up appointment. He or she may also want to refer you to other decision makers (executives or upper-level managers) at this point.

- *"I'm sorry, I'm not interested."* The executive may be saying that he or she prefers not to get involved in this matter. Or, he or she may not see a proper match between your company and the company's needs. Probe further. If the first is the case, ask to see someone else; if the second instance applies, exit gracefully. However, if you still believe the company offers a solid opportunity, try contacting another executive.

Objections from executives are often subtle. However, they are real and therefore must be handled. Perception is your best method of identifying potential problems. Remember, an objection is an opportunity either to test and qualify or to close. Design your closing to probe for the most difficult objections of all, the unstated ones. If objections are hanging around, you want to hear them. If you don't, they will still be there after you're gone.

Closing the Call

Unless the next step is clearly defined by the executive's response, end the appointment by asking questions that prompt the executive to consider what the next step should be. These questions should also invoke any still-hidden objections he or she might have regarding your company and what it is that you are offering his or her organization.

Remember, you are not selling per se; you are seeking references and endorsements. Every executive appointment will be different. Just as you have to adapt your presentation to suit the company you are calling on, you will also have to adjust your closing to fit with all that happened during your presentation.

When selecting a closing option, consider the following: How did the executive react to the information given during the discussion? Were there veiled (or conspicuous) signs of disinterest? What were the executive's direct, verbal responses to the information presented?

Here is an example of a closing question that can be used to complete your call:

If we could help your company's growth and direction by [state benefit], would it be possible to do business?

Pause and wait. Restate the question in a slightly altered form.

If we could help your company as we've talked about, what direction and advice could you give to me about how to get started?

Pause and wait as long as you have to!

If the executive's response to your close is positive, begin to sort through the details about getting started. There is a good chance that the executive will want others to hear your story. This is the time to ask for help in setting up the meetings necessary to achieve this. You want this person to set up the meeting(s) for you. Your show is on the road!

If the response is indifferent or negative, ask:

[Mr./Ms. Executive], we offer our customers [state benefit, linking it to what went over well during the discussion]. To

*evaluate correctly what we can offer to your organization, we
need your support and direction. Specifically, we need to be
introduced into [name the areas]. Would you direct me to
the appropriate management personnel?*

If the answer is yes, ask for management titles and names.
If it is no, ask if the executive would share his or her concern
with you and your manager. If you're running low on
choices, you may have to indicate that you'll find the right
people on your own, except since he already knows who
they are and has instant access to them, he could save a lot
of time for not only you, but also for them. He or she may
then decide to help . . . or to accept your challenge.

If the executive is interested, be prepared to follow up
immediately with anyone to whom you are referred, even if
that means setting up calls with eight different people. Then
keep the executive informed of your progress over time and
of any positive benefits to his or her company.

Plan to Succeed

If you expect to be successful when you call on an executive,
you must plan to succeed. The materials provided here have
been carefully developed and thoroughly tested. If you do
your homework and pick a theme that addresses your target
executive's concerns, you probably can get an appointment
about 50 percent of the time. How well you do afterwards
depends on your skill and the target company's needs. Calling high is a proven strategy that produces results for salespeople who take the time to make it work.

KEVIN'S SOLUTION

Kevin has decided that executive level calls are essential to attack
his entrenched competitor and the natural resistance to change.
After selecting the right individual on whom to call, Kevin knew that
he needed to define his product so that the big picture came

through loud and clear. One of the key parts to his story was going to be people and their productivity. His observations at McClain's many copy machine locations would give ample ammunition to make a good case.

Kevin would have to sell the concept and associated benefits of centralized reproduction clusters. Next, he would need to recognize that if McClain moved ahead, they would be prudent, and even cautious. Such a change, accompanied by significant dollar expenditures, must be supported by sure knowledge that the implementation would be both feasible and orderly. The "feasible" question would be accomplished by having the appropriate McClain people visit an installed customer site. Agreement to do this would be major call objective number one. The "orderly" part would be to survey, analyze, and document all of the procedures and processes necessary to set up a single cluster prototype within McClain Industries. To do this, Kevin would ask for one full-time McClain employee to work with him. This then, was call objective number two.

Kevin has a good plan and his approach is sound. This is a big ticket sale, and the customer must proceed with due diligence. He is making allowances for this by breaking the sale into incremental pieces. *He is also thinking like an executive!*

Kevin should keep his current activities as high as possible within McClain's management. These people have no allegiance to Kevin's competition, and while they have no reason to keep a secret, they also have no reason to explore competitive alternatives. If Kevin should inform his contacts at the user levels, he can then be sure that the competitor would become aware and be compelled to take some defensive action. Management might then elect to deal with the competitive confusion by setting up an evaluation committee, which means that all the rules would change and that nothing would happen quickly.

When calling high, your audience is likely to protect your position and the information that you have given to them. They will recognize that you have shared ideas and inside information, and have shown an unusual interest in their company. They will respect you for this and will not overtly compromise your effort. The same cannot be said for your lower-level contacts.

In Kevin's situation, it is imperative that the status quo be broken. Kevin has nothing to lose and everything to gain from his executive-level call. Only his competitor is at risk. If Kevin is successful, the competitor will fight back, but with too little and too late.

CHAPTER 7

THE SALES PROCESS

A Tough Selling Situation:

Unproductive Sales Calls

As professional salespeople, we've learned that we're not always successful in every situation. We've also developed survival techniques designed to cope with rejection and lost sales. Unproductive sales calls may be blamed on business downturns, undesirable territory assignment, competitive pressures, and so on. You must begin the sales process with the basic assumption that you aren't selling as well as you're capable, and perhaps not even as well as before! You've gravitated toward the most comfortable way of doing things and you've settled down with a set of habits that have worked for you in the past.

MIKE

Mike Thurston was constantly working but also seemed to be always running in place. He was about 80 percent of quota year-to-date and had only 10 percent of the year remaining. It was possible to achieve his goal, but only if he had good stuff already working. However, Mike admitted that his pipeline was empty. There were no prospects in the final stages of the sell cycle.

Mike reflected on two sales calls of last week. He remembered that he felt anxious and seemed to be trying too hard. He realized he hadn't really accomplished anything important on the calls. It was a tough year to be selling high ticket, high-tech products. Many businesses seemed to be holding back on major purchases. There seemed to be a general mood of caution that might last until some economic indicators turned more positive.

Mike had never had any real sales training; his company, TriMemory, didn't do much beyond product training. Mike had done some reading, but it seemed like most of it was just hype and only temporarily motivating. He knew he needed to improve his calls. In all honesty, he knew he wasn't making much of a front end investment getting ready for a call . . . and he wasn't walking away with much either. It was the fourth quarter and he could still win, but he had to execute better.

We can't subscribe to the idea that there is always a "best" way to make a sales call. We do know, however, that there is a definable process which, when consciously applied, has a high probability of making most sales calls more productive. Knowing the steps and consciously applying each step to your call situation is the only way to maximize your call productivity. This is called "sales tracking" and implies that you know where you are at any point during the call and which elements of the process still have to be completed. A sales track falls midway between a canned presentation and a completely spontaneous sales call. Both approaches have been applied successfully, but for most people an intermediate approach is generally more reliable, more consistent, and most effective over the long haul.

A canned presentation offers a logical structure and a virtual guarantee that all the important issues will be covered; however, it lacks spontaneity and flexibility. It also is ineffective for most complex products and services and is so boring that most salespeople soon modify or drop it. Even so, it's not a bad way to get started on a new product or service. Generally, a canned pitch has to overlay (rest on top of) the sales process so that the process becomes the foundation of a call or presentation. The sales track concept tells how and when to weave in and out between the canned part and the call process.

The spontaneous approach is too demanding for most salespeople, but a few extremely talented people have gotten wonderful results with it. It offers nearly unlimited freedom to use your own judgment, and it allows really talented salespeople to adjust their actions to the prospect's personality, mood, and situation. Unfortunately, most salespeople do not have the natural discipline and sensitivity to people that is needed to apply this approach successfully.

SALES TRACKING

An organized sales track is therefore a better approach for most people. It combines freedom with discipline and organization. The track ensures that each important step is taken, but the salesperson can decide how and when. You must decide the approach for each prospect, but you must also realize that no step can be completely eliminated. Dropping an apparently unnecessary step may seem efficient, but it will usually cause problems, either immediately or in the future. The following is a list of the nine sales tracking steps. Each will be developed in subsequent sections:

1. *Planning* focuses your efforts and helps you organize each sales call. You must set objectives and decide how to attain them.

2. During the *opening* you must identify yourself and your company, build rapport, capture the prospect's attention, and obtain permission to go further. This may sound easy, but realize that you will likely have only a minute to get it done. Every word said here is important.

3. *Diagnosing* means learning what the prospect's problems and situations are and how your ideas and products can solve them. People do not buy products; they buy solutions to problems. You therefore are unlikely to make the sale without learning what these problems are. Eventually you can tie your "ideas" to your products or services.

4. When *presenting*, you must directly link your product's features and benefits to your prospect's problems. You must show how you can solve these problems. However, don't be too quick. If the answer or solution is immediately apparent to you, don't spit it out. You could make your audience look foolish. Slowly massage your solution and let it surface as if it were being invented on the spot.

5. *Closing* is asking for something specific. You won't make many sales without asking for important decisions along the way; and you will increase your closing percentage if you ask frequently, take all the closing steps, use many different closing techniques, and are sensitive to buying signals.

6. Since very few people buy the first time they are asked, you must learn how to answer *objections*. Objections may be troublesome, but they should be welcomed.

They tell you what you must do to move methodically toward your call objectives.

7. *Preparing* the proposal and associated documentation should be a pleasure, but many salespeople pay little attention to it. Their carelessness costs them and their companies dearly.

8. The *courtesy close* gets you away from a recently sold prospect, thereby saving time and reducing the chances of the prospect suddenly changing to some new position.

9. *Following up* is the most neglected part of the sales track. Many salespeople feel their job is completed when the prospect has signed the order. But the salespeople who take the trouble to keep accurate records, provide after-sales service, analyze their sales calls, and plan their future calls gain an enormous competitive advantage.

Some salespeople say that planning the sales approach creates rigidity. They claim that it is better to walk in cold, size up the situation and respond to any opportunity that arises. A few successful salespeople have worked this way, but most people are effective with a track to guide them. Your plans should not be rigid or detailed. Just indicate the general approach you will use, the image you will try to create, the way you will vary your customary opening or presentation, the objections you anticipate and the way that you will respond to them, and so on.

PLANNING

Many salespeople turn a deaf ear to their manager's calls for plans. Planning bores them, and it may even look unproductive. They may claim that their time is a lot more productive when they are out in the field calling on people. There is, of course, no substitute for making calls. Some people do prepare elaborate plans and rework them time and again . . . just to avoid actually contacting prospects.

You will find that spending a few minutes on planning will make all of your calls more productive. If your management doesn't require planning, then you are well advised to initiate your own pre-call planning routine. Successful salespeople do not fly by the seats of their pants. They plan carefully and stick to their plans.

The Objective

A clear objective should be set for each sales call. You must decide what you hope to accomplish before you talk to the prospect. Without a clear objective, you could wander from one subject to another, irritate the prospect, miss opportunities, and perhaps even close the door to future business. Each objective requires a different kind of sales call. You should not use the same approach to qualify a new prospect that you use to get new opportunities from an old customer. The following are the major types of objectives:

- To qualify a new prospect

- To learn more about a qualified prospect's problems and resources

- To make a sale

- To reopen the lines of communication with an inactive customer

- To follow up on a sale

- To provide a service

The objective is so important that all your plans should be consistent with it. When your plans are complete, review them to make certain that everything fits your objective.

Results of Last Contact

Record the results of each sales call. This information will help you reopen your relationship. You can show that you are well prepared by referring directly to your last conversation and linking your current call to the prospect's situation. That kind of discipline will get the prospect's attention much more quickly than a statement of vague generalities will. The prospect will know that you have thought about him, and he will be impressed by your understanding of his interests and needs.

Type of Person

Review your previous conversations and any other information you have, then write down a few adjectives that describe the prospect: dominant, detached, or relational; young or old; cautious or impulsive; trusting or suspicious; friendly or unfriendly. You will find it is much easier to analyze a person during the planning stages than during the sales call. At call time you may be so intent on your sales track that you may neglect signals that are telling you how you must relate to this individual. So before you make the call, sit back, let your thoughts run free, and try to describe the prospect to an imaginary listener. You may find that you already know how to sell this person; you just did not consciously realize it.

Information Needed

Think about what information you will need before or during the call. Always check this just before calling to make certain you haven't forgotten something important. Few things will make you look worse than being uninformed, having forgotten something, or just not being quite ready.

THE OPENING

The opening is the sale before the sale. If you don't sell yourself in the first few moments, you will not sell your product later. The opening has four major objectives:

- To identify yourself and your company
- To capture the prospect's attention
- To open the prospect's mind
- To sell yourself

After identifying yourself and your company, these three quick steps will help you reach those objectives:

- Make a rapport-building comment.
- Make an interest-creating statement.
- Ask for permission to go further.

Each of these steps must be done confidently and professionally to create a favorable impression.

Identify Yourself and Your Company

This step is so easy and of such obvious importance that everyone should do it perfectly, but it is often omitted or performed poorly. If you doubt that assertion, just think of all the times that prospects have called you by the wrong name or asked what company you represent! There are three major reasons why this happens: speaking too rapidly, slurring over one's name, and forgetting to identify the firm properly. So speak slowly, pronounce your name clearly, and say a word or two about your company (unless you are absolutely certain that the prospect knows what your company does). Try these examples (and go slowly):

- *"Good morning. [Pause] My name is _____. I represent _____." [Pause]*

- *"Mr. Jones? [Pause for Response] My name is _____. I represent _____. We're a [Type] company." [Pause]*
- *He says, "Tom Jones here."*

  "Good morning, Mr. Jones. I'm _____. I'm here to represent _____. May I sit?"

Now try them again, and this time, smile! Be very specific about your name. We suggest you say the first name twice, followed by the last name; i.e., "My name is John—John Smith."

Keep experimenting with different combinations until you find one that communicates all the information, flows smoothly, and matches your speaking habits. Don't forget to pause; the prospect may want to say something. Don't forget to smile; a smile communicates confidence and enthusiasm—even if you are speaking on the telephone.

Make a Rapport-Building Statement

Prospects will be much more receptive to your sales message if you take a few seconds to build rapport, or a feeling of mutual understanding and communication. It can be built in many ways:

- Refer to something of which the prospect can be proud or relate to as real.

  "Mr. Jones, I read about your recent promotion to Vice President; congratulations."

  "Mr. Jones, I watched your son score two touchdowns Saturday. You must really be proud of him."

  "Mr. Jones, I've been searching for the person here who appreciates new technology and has a deep interest in productivity; and from all that I hear, you're the person."

- Refer to a mutual friend or acquaintance.

  "Mr. Jones, Bob Smith suggested that I call you."

  "Mr. Jones, I saw you last week at D'Angelo's restaurant with one of my customers, Jim Harris."

- Refer to something you have in common.

  "Mr. Jones, I see by your address that we're neighbors. I live in Woodhaven also, about four blocks from your place."

  "Mr. Jones, I've heard that you graduated from Ohio State. I got my BS there in 1984."

- Communicate understanding of the prospect's situation.

  "Mr. Jones, your secretary had to leave me on hold for a while, and I do appreciate that you're busy."

  "Mr. Jones, I know that your work keeps you very busy, so I'll be brief."

- Do not ask for permission to go further if it has already been implicitly given. Just press on.

  "Mr. Jones, we have developed and formalized several new approaches to help our customers who need to make major purchases and conserve cash at the same time. We think that the contradiction has some solutions. Could your truck fleet costs be a representative candidate?"

Skip the rapport building if the prospect is obviously rushed. For example, if you hear background noises, and the prospect is trying to talk to both you and someone else, you might say, "Mr. Jones, I wanted to talk about our approach to long-term financing with shared residual equity characteristics, but you do seem very busy. Should I call you back this afternoon, or should we reschedule for tomorrow?" If the prospect grants you permission to go further, move directly to diagnosis (or to presentation if a diagnosis is unnecessary). If you're bold, and the situation warrants, you might even suggest that he close the door.

DIAGNOSING

People do not buy products; they buy solutions to their problems. The best product in the world is worthless to them if it does not fit one of their needs. Therefore, before you present any proposal, ask yourself the critical question: What is the prospect's problem?

The Benefits of Careful Diagnosis

Careful diagnosis provides you with the information you need to make an effective presentation, and the diagnostic method improves the atmosphere and lowers the prospect's resistance.

- *Presenting the right product or service.* When you know what the prospect's problem is, you can recommend the most appropriate product or service. For example, automobile salespeople rarely analyze their prospect's needs, and they lose many sales because they concentrate on the price, options, monthly payments, and trade-in instead of learning what kind of car the prospect really needs. On the other hand, good insurance agents are very thorough analysts. They may spend two or more hours just gathering data and even more time preparing an insurance program. When they present their program, they know that it fits the prospect's needs.

- *Making the most convincing sales points.* If you do not know what the prospect needs, you can do little more than discuss your product's features and make a few general statements about the benefits to the prospect. If you have made a thorough diagnosis, you can link your sales points directly to your prospect's needs and problems. For example, as a sales representative presenting your product, you might respond to concerns about costs by addressing how the change in associated functions adds value in very real ways. Be specific; vague statements will not erase the concern.

- *Creating a mutual problem-solving atmosphere.* Careful, tactful diagnosis will reduce the prospect's sales resistance and change the atmosphere from conflict to cooperation. People do not like to be sold. However, the same person who strenuously resists salespeople will often be glad to discuss his or her problems with a sympathetic listener. Many people are starved for understanding. They feel that nobody really cares. If you communicate that you want to understand, most people will be willing to talk to you.

- *Increasing the prospects' receptivity.* If you listen to them, they will listen to you. It is as simple as that. There is a natural tendency to behave toward people the way they behave toward us. Since you have tried to understand them, they will try to understand you.

- *Making more sales calls.* Why don't salespeople make that extra call? Because selling is a lonely business. Every time you contact a prospect, you risk rejection. Diagnostic selling lowers resistance and changes the atmosphere. Instead of an adversary to be resisted, you are a welcome problem solver. When you begin to know that you can achieve this status, it will help you to make that extra call.

Information-Gathering Techniques
You can't make a diagnosis without information, but many people do not want to talk to you—at least not at the start. If you ask direct questions, some people will answer them,

but many people will resent your "invasion of their privacy." You haven't earned the right to be so direct.

Your first task, therefore, is to get the prospect to talk, even if he or she does not discuss exactly what you need to know. No matter what is said, you will learn something about his or her situation and personality. Once prospects are talking, it is fairly easy to change the subject. The ice is broken; they have learned that you listen and they will respond positively to gentle attempts to change the subject.

People will generally resist even the gentlest questions until you have given them some information. You have contacted them and it is up to you to make the first move. You should begin by making a few remarks that amplify your ingenious attention-creating statement, then ask an open-ended question such as, "What do you think of that?" or "Does that sound at all interesting?" Open-ended questions ask for the prospect's opinions, attitudes, and feelings. They invite a long and far-ranging response. The prospect may go far beyond your immediate question and discuss many other issues.

Once a few open-ended questions have gotten the prospect talking freely, active listening will sustain the momentum. Active listening has been called "listening with the third ear." You have two ears to hear words with, but you need an inner ear to hear the subtle meanings. People rarely talk in a completely frank manner. They drop hints, shrug, raise or lower their voices, and send you distorted messages. Listen actively: go beyond the words, try to relate each statement to previous ones, and look for non-verbal messages. You will learn a great deal and impress the prospect with your ability to understand. There are six steps to effective, *active* listening:

- *Concentrate.* Talk in a quiet voice and, if you can, in a quiet place. Put your own problems aside and concentrate all your attention on the prospect.

- *Shut up.* If you are talking, he or she can't.

- *Never interrupt.* Interrupting not only prevents you from learning what the prospect was going to say, it also irritates the prospect and closes his or her mind. (Exceptions to this are noted in Chapter 5.)

- *Use silence.* A long pause invites a person to speak. (Don't over-do it, as it can be interpreted as a challenge.)

- *Keep your mind open.* Don't jump to conclusions or evaluate the prospect in "right/wrong" or "good/bad" terms. You can miss what was meant, and you may also offend the other person, who may say, in effect, "What right do you have to sit in judgment of me or my comments?"

- *Show you understand.* In your own words, restate points the prospect made. Link a statement to earlier positions. Pick up subtle hints and make them explicit. From time to time, summarize the overall pattern you have heard. When prospects feel that you are "tuned in," they will talk much more freely and objectively.

More important, if you do not understand, such a summary invites the prospect to correct you. Some salespeople are afraid to admit they don't understand, but these fears are irrational. People do not lose respect for someone who communicates that she or he is trying to understand but is having difficulty doing so. On the contrary, they appreciate the interest and openness and do whatever they can to clarify their positions.

Open-ended questions and active listening will create a good atmosphere and provide a great deal of information, but you will still need to learn additional specific facts. In that case, closed-ended questions are most appropriate. Closed-ended questions can be answered "yes" or "no" or with a specific number or bit of information.

Integrating the Techniques

Each technique has advantages and disadvantages. Active listening provides the maximum amount of information and usually makes the largest improvement in your relationship with the prospect. But much of this information may be irrelevant; the technique takes a great deal of time; you will not control this part of the call; and some prospects will be irritated by the slow pace and lack of structure.

Open-ended questions offer some of the advantages of the two extreme types. They provide more control than active listening and obtain more information than closed-ended questions. They generally improve the atmosphere. Again, your price is time and control!

Closed-ended questions give you the maximum degree of control, and they often provide exactly the information you need. However, they do not provide important information that you do not request. They can also irritate some prospects, particularly when you ask several closed-ended questions in a short period of time. Prospects may feel that they are being cross-examined and turn completely off.

Unfortunately, many salespeople are so intent on controlling the interview that they rely almost exclusively on closed-ended questions. If they ask an open-ended one, they may not hear the entire answer to it. In fact, they may interrupt the prospect when he or she starts to go beyond the specific information the salesperson wants.

A really professional salesperson can use all three techniques and switch from one to another as purposes and the prospect's mood changes. When you want to stimulate talking, give up control and encourage the prospect to talk with open-ended questions and active listening. When you need specific information again, ask closed-ended questions.

Study the prospect's face, gestures, and posture to see the kind of response achieved by each of your techniques. If the prospect dislikes open-ended questions and an unclear structure, you must become more directive and ask specific questions. If the prospect likes to talk, you need to become more passive and go with the flow. By shifting tactics, you not only learn more, you also communicate to the prospect that you are hearing and responding to his or her needs and mood. This subtle message improves both the information flow and the general atmosphere.

Conclusion

Techniques are much less important than intentions. If you are sincerely interested in understanding your prospect's problems, your concern will be recognized, and almost any technique will do. If you communicate insincerity, no technique can accomplish much. You must concentrate all of your attention on answering that critical question: What is the prospect's problem and how am I reacting to it?

Check your diagnosis with the prospect. If you agree on the problem, you can easily make an effective presentation. If you don't agree, you must continue probing until you know what the prospect thinks the problem is. The prospect's ideas may not be the ones you would have in the same situation, but they are the ones that determine the reactions to your proposal. You must therefore adjust your presentation to fit her or his beliefs or continue your conversation until you observe a change in those beliefs.

PRESENTING

Presenting your story clearly and attractively is certainly important, but it cannot compensate for an inability to establish rapport, diagnose, answer objections, and close. By all means sharpen your presentation skills, but do not become so concerned with what you are saying that you ignore the important person—the prospect.

Set a Clear Objective

Your presentation will accomplish more if you follow a few simple rules: Know exactly what you want the prospect to do after you make this presentation. Go beyond glittering generalities like "buy." Set specific objectives such as delivery schedules, the terms, the improvement in your relationship, and so on. Then make sure that what you say and what the prospect hears is completely consistent with your objective.

Organize Your Presentation

A good presentation has a clear organization with a well-defined beginning, middle, and end. The opening provides an overview of what you will discuss. It tells the prospect where you are going and helps her or him to follow you. You might say,

"Mr. Fisher, today I want to review my understanding of how your company builds toward the actual ordering process and then ask you to highlight any key parts that I may be missing. And then, Mr. Fisher, I'm going to ask you about how you sort through the financial options and relate them to any imposed budget constraints."

The body provides detailed information about each major topic. To help the prospect understand the flow, you should briefly introduce each new subject. This is a good time to recall our earlier discussions on linkage and building bridges in Chapter 5. Be careful not to jump to the body; rather, verbally walk across your bridge with the prospect by your side. For clarification, the body of your call will have several key elements, and they will all have linkage to each other, for example:

"We have seen how this plan can ease the administrative process; and, if you feel comfortable with that, we can look at the scheduling implications. Are there any questions? Do you feel comfortable with the administrative process? Okay, let's move on to monitoring and hitting delivery requirements."

The summary pulls it together and restates the major benefits:

> *"Mr. Fisher, today we've been able to match our program features to your concerns about the just-in-time effort here at Republic National Systems. In many ways, I think you'll agree, it is almost as if our company designed this program for you! Some budget constraints you mentioned were new for me, but I think we can go a long way toward accommodating them."*

The Close Is the Pay-off

A presentation without a close is a wasted effort. Once you have summarized the benefits, ask for one of the call objectives you originally had in mind or that you now need because of new information:

> *"Mr. Fisher, I can see that the overall acquisition methods are going to be a key part of RNS's decision and, in that regard, I'm going to ask for a special favor. You can appreciate that the better informed I am, the more on target our proposal will be. The favor is simply an introduction to Mr. Milt Friedman, your Director of Materials and Controls. Will you please do that for me?"*

A clearly organized presentation moves smoothly toward a natural close. A disorganized presentation generally accomplishes nothing at all because your audience is confused. At the end, you're on the last page and they are somewhere else.

Keep It Short

If you talk too long, the prospect can easily turn off. If you do not say enough, the prospect will ask for any information he or she needs or provide some other opportunity for you to make additional comments. So set an absolute minimum time for your presentation and then make sure that you keep on schedule.

Emphasize Benefits

Your prospects are much less interested in the product itself than in what it can do for them. They care about its benefits, not its features. A feature is a characteristic of the product or service. For example, a TV set's features might include a 25-inch screen, 100 percent solid state construction and instant start-up.

A benefit is the value that a feature provides to the prospect. Features do not vary, but benefits do. The same product may offer different benefits to different prospects because they have different needs. For example, the fact that a baby's highchair can be folded would be an important benefit to someone who plans to take it on trips. It has no value at all to someone who intends to keep it in one place. In fact, folding might be regarded as a negative feature because the chair has less stability.

Let's return to the TV set example. The 25-inch screen means that you can watch from any part of a large room. One hundred percent solid state increases reliability and lowers service costs. Instant start-up saves you the time and boredom of waiting for the set to warm up. Each of these benefits will be more attractive to the prospect if the salesperson dramatizes them:

"You know how boring it is to wait for the set to warm up; you stand there for a minute or so, but it seems like an hour. With this set, you don't wait at all."

Most sales presentations emphasize features, not benefits. Salespeople generally know much more about their products than they do about their customers. It is easy to talk about 350 horsepower or 99 percent uptime. But prospects are much less interested in these features than they are in rapid acceleration and safety while passing, or more dependable operation.

If you have made an adequate diagnosis, you can stress the benefits that most interest your prospect. Your presentation will be particularly effective if you stress its advantages over any current plans or the other possibilities under consideration. Advantages are benefits the other plan does not provide. The more directly you compare your proposal's benefits to those offered elsewhere, the better your chances of making the sale.

Encourage a Dialogue

Many salespeople are afraid of questions and comments. They brush them off by saying, "I'm glad you asked that. I'll cover it later." Then they probably never get back to it. Of course, you can't answer every question and still keep organized, but a back-and-forth exchange—even a disorganized one—is more likely to produce results than a brilliant monologue.

Pause from time to time and ask for reactions . . . and be sensitive to nonverbal messages. If the prospect indicates approval, go full speed ahead. If he or she seems confused, dubious or annoyed, find out why; then change your emphasis, language, tone, or pace. In other words, during the presentation you must concentrate on the same issues as at every other step in the sales process—the prospect's needs and problems. It is important to present your product clearly and attractively, but it is infinitely more important to understand the prospect's problems, emphasize those benefits that apply, and adjust to the prospect's reactions as you encounter them.

CLOSING

Perhaps the greatest mistake that a salesperson can make is to fail to ask for the order or for something important. Many salespeople make that mistake several times a day. They fail to move ahead because they are afraid to ask for something special. They don't want to change their pleasant chat into a real sales call. But most prospects do not want to chat with you; they want you to do your job. They dislike time-wasters and respect salespeople with the self-confidence and professionalism to ask for their business.

Most of them also appreciate your help in making decisions. They realize that they tend to procrastinate and want a little push in the right direction. In other words, the best way to keep people's respect is also the only way to make your living. Every time you present your solution, ask for a commitment.

OVERCOMING OBJECTIONS

As you go through the sales call steps, you will get questions and objections. They are a necessary part of a call and offer times for you to make your strongest points. Some salespeople are afraid of objections, but the real professionals welcome them. An objection tells you what you must do next. You must overcome reluctance to act now, correct misunderstandings, remove doubts, suggest a different product, or stress your product's benefits and advantages.

There are four major steps to overcoming objections: Clarifying, Classifying, Answering, and Restating Benefits and Moving Ahead.

Clarifying

The basic technique is to restate the objection as a question, then pause for the prospect's reaction. The question need not be asked directly. Your tone or manner of pausing may imply that you are asking a question:

- *"You think that contracts that extend over three years are somewhat of a risk then, is that true? [Pause and Listen] Would you explain the policy objectives for me?" [Pause and Listen Closely]*

- "I think that you may believe that the rates are higher than you would pay to our competitor. [Pause, If there is no response, Ask . . .] Do you feel that way?"

- "If I understand you correctly, you are concerned that the components may be unreliable and expensive to maintain. Is that about how you feel?" [The Response] "What would it take to convince you otherwise?"

Change your words often ("you think," "you feel," "if I read you correctly," "you may want," "you seem to want," "you don't appear to like"), but follow the same form of restating the objection in slightly different words. You may ask or imply that you would like to know if your understanding is correct. This method has four valuable effects:

- Your question and pause gently force the prospect to indicate whether your understanding is correct. If you do understand, you can classify and answer the objection. If you are confused, the prospect will probably tell you so and reword the objection more clearly. You can then classify and respond to it.

- You show the prospect that you take the objection seriously and want to understand his position. That is, you communicate respect for the prospect, which increases rapport and confidence in you.

- Your respect and desire to understand will cause many prospects to tell you what they really think. They will become less defensive, more willing to be open and objective. For example, a client might admit that she is not really concerned about what you're asking for, but is concerned about the *implications* of what you're asking for.

- You show respect and a desire to understand without reinforcing objections by agreeing with them. There is a vast difference between saying, "You think the price is too high," and saying, "The price is too high." The first shows respect for the prospect, but does not concede that the objection is correct. The second can increase the prospect's belief that the price really is too high.

For all these reasons, when a prospect objects, your first step should be to restate the objection as a question, then wait for a response. You must confirm that the objection was a real one and then you must get it rounded out to understand it fully. There isn't any other sure way for you to frame a good response, or one that is on target and has a good chance of being accepted.

Classifying

Since each type of objection requires a different kind of answer, you should classify objections before answering them. Don't spurt out your impulsive thought, although you may be exactly on target. It was your prospect's objection, so handle it respectfully. The following are the four classes of objections:

- A **stall** is any reason given to postpone action. "I want to think it over." "I have to discuss it with [whomever]." "I'll call you back." "I want to wait until after Christmas," etc. Some stalls are legitimate, but many of them are rationalizations. People are afraid to act, but cover up their fears with plausible yet insincere stalls, thereby avoiding painful decisions while preserving their belief that they are really strong and decisive.

- A **hidden objection** is concealed beneath the surface of another objection. For example, many stalls cover up more basic objections. It is much easier to say, "I'd like to wait until after Christmas," than to say, "I don't trust you" or, "I think your company gives poor service" or, "I'm not authorized to make this kind of decision."

There are three reliable indicators that a prospect has hidden objections: (1) illogical objections, (2) large numbers of objections, particularly inconsistent ones, and (3) refusals to accept good answers to objections. When you encounter any of these signs, there are probably hidden objections. If you encounter two or three of these signs, hidden objections are a near certainty.

- An **easy objection** is one based on a misunderstanding or lack of information. These objections are often requests for information, even if they are not stated as a question. An example is: "Your payment terms seem unusual."

- A **hard objection** indicates a desire for a benefit that your product does not offer. An example is: "We don't do business with suppliers who don't offer early payment discounts."

Answering

Each type of objection requires a different kind of answer. This is why classification is so important.

- When the prospect stalls, stress the value of prompt action and the dangers of procrastination. It could be as simple as, "You know we can't get to step two if we hang here forever on step one."

- When you sense that the prospect has a hidden objection, probe for it. However, you must not probe until after you have answered the stated objection—even if you are convinced that it is just a cover-up. Ignoring it communicates disrespect and closes the prospect's mind. He becomes even more resistant to telling you what he really thinks. So answer the stated objection briefly, then probe for the underlying objections.

- When the prospect raises an easy objection, just provide the necessary information. If possible, provide objective evidence to support your position.

- When the prospect raises a hard objection, minimize the missing benefit and stress the benefits your product does offer.

Restating Benefits and Closing

Each time you have completely answered an objection, test to make sure that the prospect accepts your answer, then restate the benefits—particularly the key ones—and take the opportunity to move the call ahead. Do not be afraid of boring the prospect. Prospects want to know what your product can do for them, and it can take several repetitions to get the message across. Furthermore, restating the benefits shifts the prospect's attention from the objection to the merits of your proposal.

FOLLOWING UP

The whole process of Account Development requires that follow-up be timely, consistent, and in response to all promises and commitments. Even little touches can make the difference between a satisfied customer and one who is annoyed to the extent that he or she would just as soon not see you again . . . and even may pass these feelings on to associates.

To the customer, you are the company. We live in a cynical age, and many people distrust salespeople and even corporations. Too many people feel that, "Salespeople just want your money; once they have it, you never see them again—until the next time they want your business." These feelings present both a threat and an opportunity. If you do not follow up, you will reinforce their cynicism. "He's just like all the rest of them; he grabbed our deal and ran away." These feelings cause people to nitpick, to take their business to somebody else, to downgrade you and your company to their friends, and perhaps even to get out of their present obligations.

On the other hand, since so many salespeople do not follow up, you have a wonderful opportunity. You can stand out. People will see you as a person who cares, as one who gives the personal service they long for. If you provide continuing, cheerful liaison between your customers and your company, they will be more satisfied with your products and services, and be much more likely to buy again and to recommend you to their friends. This is a key to effective account management.

Analyzing Sales Calls

A different type follow-up can improve your sales techniques—regular analysis of successful and unsuccessful calls. If you made a sale, why did they buy? What did you do right? How is that different from other approaches you have used? If you struck out, what did you do wrong? What could you do differently in the future?

An edge can be lost at any point in the sales process—even during the planning stages or because you did not follow up after a previous meeting. You should therefore analyze every step you took or failed to take. The following checklist will help you recognize what you do well and what areas need improvement.

I.   Planning

    A.   Did you have a clear objective?

    B.   Did you have all the information you needed, including information about the prospect's personality?

    C.   What could you have done better?

II. Opening

    A. Did you clearly identify yourself and your firm?

    B. Did you establish rapport?

    C. Did you make an interest-creating statement?

    D. Did you request permission to go further?

    E. Think about what you could have done better.

III. Diagnosing

    A. Did you discover and discuss your understanding of the prospect's problem?

    B. Did the prospect agree with your diagnosis?

    C. Did you obtain all the information you needed to make an accurate diagnosis?

    D. How could you have done better?

IV. Presenting

    A. Did you summarize the prospect's problem?

    B. Did you create and clearly show how your product or services could solve that problem?

    C. Did you focus on needs and benefits more than product features?

    D. What could you have done better?

V. Closing

    A. Did you earn the right to ask for something important?

    B. Did you ask for it?

    C. Did you read buying or agreement signals?

    D.   What could you have done better?

VI. Overall Evaluation

    A.   How satisfied are you with your performance?

    B.   When was the essence of the call made or lost?

    C.   What should you do differently the next time you contact this person?

    D.   What might you do differently with another person?

Planning Your Next Contact

Immediately after each call you should plan your next contact with the prospect. Their situations and personality will never be clearer than they are right after the call, so note when you will contact each person, what you will try to accomplish, how you will alter your approach, and so on. It will take only a few minutes to make these plans, and doing so will automatically increase your production. You will call on the right people, at the right time, with the right product, and the right sales approach. How can you miss?

Understanding the sales process is key to your success and may require frequent review of this material. Therefore, as a quick reference, we have developed an outline summarizing this information, which can be found in the Appendix.

MIKE'S SOLUTION

Mike needed a working tool, so he developed a chart that was essentially a Sales Call Planner outlining five key components:

1. Account Name and Department

2. Situation

3. Things to Accomplish

4. Logic and Strategies to Use

5. Key Issues

Mike carried out his new technique during a call on Doug Smithers, who had been assigned to study future resource requirements in his company's Information Services facilities. Mike knew only that Doug had moved up through the financial side of the business. From this viewpoint, Mike established an overriding goal for this call—to convince Doug that TriMemory had products that could increase central computer performance and greatly extend the life of already installed equipment—without compromising quality in any way. New mainframes were no longer the only way to move to higher levels of computer power. Other solutions were available that could also delay large capital outlays for as long as two years.

The next step was to assure Doug that TriMemory could prove the soundness of add-on memory and refurbished channel hardware. This was a financially based decision and one that the end-user groups would not buy into; therefore, after Doug bought into the idea as a viable option, Mike had to ask Doug for his opinion about how this solution could be carried out at the user/buyer level.

Mike explained that he knew something about the bottleneck being caused by hardware limitations in the four primary Information Services facilities. He suggested that the traditional solution, and the one always proposed by manufacturers of mainframe equipment, was to replace and upgrade. This path left everyone happy and safe . . . except perhaps the "keeper" of the company's balance sheet.

Mike was building a bridge to link this opening to the body of the call. He said that some companies saw this as a two-dimensional problem where you could either struggle with the computer power dilemma, or you could fix it and accept the financial impact. Mike said, "Mr. Smithers, is this a reasonable description, and what additional dimensions do you see?"

Doug helped him finish the bridge as he replied, "If I accepted the two-dimensional conclusion, then I wouldn't even want to spend time looking at this problem. I can't buy the idea that you are damned if you do and damned if you don't. My job is to sort through this problem and to find the other dimensions of it. Simply stated, we do have to solve the bottleneck problem and minimize the financial impact at the same time."

Mike knew where he was on the sales track. He saw that the bridge was complete; all he needed to do was to validate and check that he had permission to go on. "Doug, I think you're out to find and measure other alternatives, and it follows that if we can show you one or more proven solutions, then you'll want to listen to them, is that true?"

Doug replied, "Yes, I still consider this whole thing to be in the investigative stages. Lets hear about your options."

Mike was over the bridge and into the presentation, or body, part of his call. He used a chart illustrating the impact channel speeds could have on downloading data via wide area networks to remote work stations. *He presented, bridged, validated, and moved ahead.* Doug Smithers clearly accepted that the TriMemory approach had merit, and he wanted to pursue these new options.

There remained the very sensitive issues surrounding the second objective of this call. Mike said, "My discussions with your colleagues in Information Services and Purchasing seem to suggest that they are getting geared up to move out on the single solution of upgrading with all new replacement hardware. I've been unable to get them to listen to the opportunities we've been talking about here. Doug, I think this is a real problem and something that I can do very little about."

Doug Smithers not only took the bait, he seemed to relish it. He said it was already known that those people weren't looking at all sides of the problem. He could and would insure that premature decisions or commitments were not made. He asked Mike if he could put together several of the comparison charts they had looked at along with some descriptive narrative . . . not a full-blown proposal but just a tool to work with for the moment.

Mike agreed and then did a bold thing. He asked if Doug could help him meet with Carl Sommers, VP of Administrative Services. He explained that a large segment of the end users fell under Mr. Sommers' domain and therefore a sizable portion of the Information Services expenditures finally found their way back to Mr. Sommers' budget, but that he had been unable to get an appointment with him. Doug said that he'd arrange for Carl to join them when Mike returned with the chart package.

After the call, Mike thought about what had happened. He knew it had been a productive call. All three objectives were met and follow-up activities were being scheduled. He had made real progress today and was feeling very good.

———————————

CHAPTER 8

THE SPECIAL SALES CALL

A Tough Selling Situation:
Fickle Buyers and Ungrateful Users

The business you currently have from your customer may appear volatile and subject to an uncertain future. Buyers don't treat you or your products as special. Some seem to put up with you and they don't convey that they need you. It's tough to sell when you sense that they don't care. Go into your accounts and practice the lessons in this chapter and then your customers will have reason to care!

KEITH

Keith forced himself to take an insightful assessment of his territory. He had 23 accounts that generated the bulk of his annual revenue. To the best of his knowledge, he was sole supplier in 8 of those accounts and shared the remaining 15 with one or more competitors. Keith knew that in his industry, such sharing was not unusual. He also knew that each competitor was constantly on the hunt to increase its share . . . and at the expense of other suppliers. They had the same contacts he had, and Keith often saw their literature lying on someone's desk.

It was an uncertain world, and a buyer could become fickle at any time. He wished that they would develop more appreciation for the quality of his product and for his personal support services. Keith didn't believe that any of the competitors gave better account service than he did. Realistically, he reasoned that there were customers who wouldn't agree and, likewise, some buyers and users probably felt more comfortable with one of the competitor's salespeople. Keith deduced that he needed to attack a potentially bad situation before it happened. He labeled it an "erosion because of fickle buyers and users."

Many tough selling situations can spill out of an account where the salesperson has fragile business relationships with the users and buyers. The presence of these weak and non-supportive relationships will cause selling frustrations and gradual loss of sales to a competitor. It is counterproductive to suggest that the buyers and users will "come around" if the salesperson does more of the same. It is more productive to realize that the seller has built fragile relationships and must take ownership of and responsibility for them.

Users and buyers can be cultivated and should become committed to one supplier's product and services over other suppliers with similar products. Achieving this level of support will take time, effort, planning and skillful selling techniques. In short, changing the characteristics of business relationships will require a consequential investment. Some assigned accounts warrant such an investment, while others may have limited potential that cannot justify a concentrated effort. In Chapter 11, we will show you how to evaluate and justify selling investments. But our focus here assumes that the salesperson has cause to want to enhance account relationships and has decided to make whatever investments may be required.

The answer lies in the *Special Sales Call*. The special sales call must be repeated with numerous customer contacts. It must be made on *executives, operating managers*, and on *users and buyers*. The objective of a special sales call is to establish the salesperson as a knowledgeable problem solver who has a keen interest in helping the customer successfully use her or his products and services. You should be more than a peddler. These calls are *special* because each audience is carefully selected and because the call content is customized to satisfy the functional interests of each audience.

The special sales call should be the most important thing you do. Everything has to come together during the call. Whether you're calling high, low, or just making a call, this is where you should demonstrate all that you are and all that you know. In some fashion, which may not be obvious to you, this is where you are graded; if you accomplish anything, this is where it will happen.

In business-to-business selling, you must make lots of calls—there is no substitute. You must make these calls on customers that you already have, customers you don't know, and prospects who don't do any business with you. You must make them on accounts committed to your competition and into accounts where you haven't been welcomed.

Ungrateful users aren't necessarily ungrateful people. People need a reason to show appreciation and to have any degree of allegiance to you as a supplier. Salespeople have to earn these rewards. The best way to do that is to make responsible calls and to become involved in anything related to your product.

YOUR CALL TARGET

We talk about numerous "call levels" in this book. When you are providing good territory coverage, that usually means lower-level call activity. When you are making, or maintaining an account development effort, you will accelerate your coverage and you will extend your contacts horizontally and vertically throughout the organization. Account development means that your call activity is extending to include management, upper management, and executive calls. Additionally, when you are engaged in account development activities, where applicable, you will be expanding your contacts and business relationships into more departments and divisions within the company. Here, you will use your activity in one department to link to new activity in another department and so on.

Many companies have multiple divisions, and account development will include an objective to penetrate into these additional divisions. Larger companies may also be segmented into different "businesses." This may have resulted from sheer growth, mergers, acquisitions, and so on. Your account development efforts look at all of these linkages to determine applicability for your products and services. The next activity is to begin plans and tactics to make these "businesses" part of your account.

High Calls

Let's focus on "call levels" within all these possibilities. Account development activities do not exclude calls at any level. Both low levels and high levels, in any specific situation, may be extremely important call targets. But low or high does have something to do with the subject matter of your call content. Low or high for our purposes has more to do with the job function in contrast to the job title. Titles used at one company may be deceiving, while in another company, they may be very descriptive. For example, one vice president may be a hands-on person who understands and controls most every facet of his organizational responsibilities. Another vice president, even in the same company, may delegate consequential activities to lieutenants. A call on either of the above vice presidents is a high level call, but they should be handled very differently. Getting an appointment with either is going to require a strong story.

The hands-on vice president is likely to answer his own phone. You'll get his secretary only if his line is busy or he is in conference. This vice president is on the phone often because he is sending out orders while inspecting results of previously sent orders. This vice president seems to have a short attention span, but in reality he has such a grasp of everything that is going on, only update information is required. All the background data are already known. Your call for an appointment will be quickly dispatched. You'll either get it, be delegated immediately, or be told that he has no interest, and that no one else in the group will be interested either.

The delegating vice president seems to have more time but will be more likely to want to set you up with a lieutenant. Still, this vice president may elect to see you to better understand which lieutenant should subsequently hear your whole story.

It is interesting to think about what will happen given two identical situations controlled by the vice president types described above. The chances are that your objective win/lose odds are about the same. Their conclusions will most often be the same, as each will arrive at the correct solution. With the hands-on vice president, you'll know in a heartbeat. With the delegating vice president, it'll take a while and numerous sales calls on the lieutenants.

Senior Management Targets

You may seldom have the opportunity to call on a company CEO. You may get occasional shots at some senior executives. There are similarities between them.

The typical CEO is a white, married (never divorced) male, 57 years old. He and his wife's three children have graduated from college and are out into the world. His wife most likely was a homemaker but is now into more volunteer work and sponsorship. They are Protestant and conservative. They are reluctant to change homes, and the one they have is too large for them. On average, he will spend 20 hours in company meetings each week and will attend weekend meetings at least once a month. He will often have after-hours business meetings and will be out of town one or two weeks each month. The CEO is much in demand by the community at large. He tries to be too much to too many.

The senior executives are white, married males ranging from 48 to 53. They, too, are mostly Protestant and may have children still in college. They were more likely to have grown up in a medium-sized midwest city. They work hard and also work long hours. They are still holding tightly to a strong desire to achieve and display lots of energy and enough desire to use it up. About half these guys have been with their company for 15 to 20 years. Three-quarters of them have worked for only two or three companies. These senior executives believe in hard work, family, education, and honesty. They are mostly conservative on financial issues as well as social issues. Only about 10 percent are related to an influential director, stockholder, or company official. Most are found to be very pleasant, courteous human beings. They are at ease and convey that they are not threatened. Should you get an appointment with one of the senior executives within your account, don't be too surprised. Some yearn for an occasional diversion. This executive will make you feel at ease and will listen attentively to everything you say . . . unless you don't have anything to say.

It's important that you remember that as you go about getting the appointment, you're going to have to pass through the secretarial gate (a filter). So any topics you plan to use must be synthesized to convince the secretary that you warrant consideration for time on the boss's calendar.

Following are some ideas about potential conversations that might interest some of your "call high" targets.

Upper Management Conversation Topics

The call content at the upper management level is going to have to be different; you have to remove yourself from product emphasis. There are exceptions, but they are not typical. Most products have indirect, and less obvious peripheral attributes and implications. The professional salesperson making upper management calls must give considerable thought to this and develop techniques to give substance to these attributes.

When businesses buy products or services, they are trying to meet a need and/or solve a problem. It follows that your product or service meets a need generated by a business requirement, a business problem, or a business opportunity. The upper management types won't care much about your product, but they will have an interest in *the requirement, the problem,* or *the opportunity.* This must become your focus to warrant the appointment with upper level managers.

Suppose a customer had annual expenditures of over $100,000 for your product. If amounts already being spent are noteworthy, you may be considered an important supplier to this customer. You already have a business relationship; you and your products help this customer in doing business. Suppose the annual expenditure didn't seem to be large enough to attract attention based on past years. Your statement might be: "Since I have served your company, you've spent over a quarter million dollars with my company. That would qualify us as an important supplier to your company." Upper management types know the importance of suppliers who perform well. Without them their own business would experience difficulties.

A change of ownership, or any other consequential organizational change may be either important or interesting to your customer's management. If you are also a current supplier, then so much the better. Executive changes, reorganizations, mergers, acquisitions, and so on are topics of general interest among upper management types.

Technology is a good springboard into the executive offices, if you can relate it to an issue that he or she feels is important. The following four items suggest how your statements could include issues that stimulate interest with certain upper management types, yet would have little value at the user or buyer level.

- ... and this could displace many people in companies like yours.

- ... and such legislation will be bad for companies like mine, and perhaps like yours.

- ... and the retraining costs are going to put pressures on many companies.

- ... and the Centralized Reproduction Clusters forces us to look at documents labeled "company private" in new ways.

An appeal that usually works is the request for understanding and/or direction. "I represent a company with a product line that should at least warrant consideration by your company, but I can't seem to find a decision maker or understand how your company evaluates new ideas." This is a one-way appeal and, while it may do the trick, it begs for an exchange. Surely there must be a little something you can barter with. You could describe how another of your accounts is achieving some specific objective.

Customized Selling in the High Sales Call

Salespeople have a responsibility to redefine their product in terms that are not inherently obvious within the product itself. This is sometimes called *concept selling* versus tangible selling. Use the points below as a guide to create a customized list to help describe your product in a new and more exciting way:

- enhances quality of your operations,
- frees up resources (people or other),
- offers job enrichment opportunity,
- simplifies tasks,
- is accompanied by value-added services,
- can have positive side effects,
- conserves your cash flow,
- nourishes a partnership relationship.

To test your ability to somehow disguise a product and make it saleable, try the following scenario:

Suppose you sold envelopes for a living. No business wants to buy envelopes, but they all have to do it. Think of the envelopes that arrive at your home each week. You have seen the two-way envelope that, when opened in a certain way and carefully refolded and glued in a prescribed fashion, miraculously becomes the out-going envelope for your order or payment. Who are the business people who would buy these envelopes? More interesting, what did the salesperson say to convince someone that this was a great deal? *User friendly* was probably not used as a selling benefit or advantage. Let's consider what the salesperson might have sold:

- One-pass computer preparation, therefore less handling, which reduces people time and associated costs.

- Return envelope not needed; therefore cost of that envelope is eliminated and a stuffing procedure is bypassed.

- Advanced envelope technology . . . everyone will be going this way.

- Inventory reductions because only one item is stocked.

- Potential reduction in mailing cost.

- Higher return because the bill and the return envelope never become separated.

Firming Up Your Special Sales Call Appointment

There are many demands on upper management types. Many people want some of their time, and the executive's calendar changes frequently. You're penciled in there, but you are also the easiest to scratch out. It makes sense to immediately follow up with a confirmation letter with a brief agenda enclosed. One as simple as the following example will do the job:

Dear Mr. Benton:

I am looking forward to our meeting in your office on [date] at [time]. At that time I want to share how my company's products are used in two of my customer's facilities. Their application is innovative, and I believe it could have merit in your company.

Afterward, I hope that you will give me advice and direction about where, to whom, and how I might introduce our capabilities into [company name].

Mr. Benton, I appreciate the value of your time as well as your agreeing to see me on [day of week]. I have organized my message to be concise and to the point as outlined in the enclosed agenda.

Cordially,

Your confirmation letter and your agenda help take the curse off this call. The executive may have thought that your time slot on his calendar gave him some last minute flexibility. Your letter and agenda make it somewhat difficult for him to procrastinate at the last moment.

Sponsorship

Upper management types do not confer a direct sponsorship status on your future activities within an account, nor do they require subordinates to do anything in your behalf. Sponsorship is the subtle *support gained in your upper management call.* It will often be suggested that you could tell your story to a specific subordinate executive. The executive's secretary might even be an accomplice in helping you to arrange that next meeting.

At least several factors will support the "idea" that you have sponsorship. First, you did see and talk to this key executive, and you didn't get thrown out. The executive did make certain suggestions, if only to call on someone else. You are much more likely to get a reasonable audience because of this suggestion (and its source) than if you did not have it.

Further, subtle sponsorship is achieved by your astute handling of the second call. If played properly, you should get an opportunity for a third executive level call. By this time, whether or not you actually have sponsorship is becoming a moot issue. As your call activities move downward within the organization, it will appear as though someone must be sponsoring you . . . and you will act that way!

As you pursue additional call activity within the account, you will have the opportunity to tell other contacts something about the upper level calls that you have made. This is good leverage and tends to cause the current contact to listen more closely. This new contact (or an old contact engaged in a new conversation) is likely to think that you told the same story upstairs and there was at least tacit approval about what you said. If it were not so, you wouldn't still be here bringing it up again. Imagine the reaction to a salesperson who says the following:

"When I spoke to Mr. Calhoun (three levels up) he seemed surprised that the company hadn't already looked at this. I did explain that your group seemed either quite busy or understaffed; but, frankly, Jack, he didn't seem to accept either

. . . and then your name came up as perhaps the right person to look at this idea. Do you think that you could find the time to work with me on this?"

Jack's response could take any of several directions. The smart salesperson didn't relate the above conversation with Mr. Calhoun without having anticipated Jack's alternatives.

Your upper level calls should be designed so that you are enabled to gain leverage as you continue toward your sales objectives. In order to do this, and while you're making the upper level call, you must create the impression that you are more than a "seller." You want the executive to begin getting the impression that you are a businessperson. To the extent that you are able to do this during the call, the executive will be inclined to ask for more information and will also feel more comfortable in giving you information.

If you have been working at your account coverage objectives, it is likely that you have seen or otherwise learned of things that are unknown at upper levels. Most times, you might be well advised to keep quiet, but there are times when you must make a move. If the information is important, but is not related to you as a "seller," it may be appreciated and may also enhance the "business person" characteristic. Here is an example:

Jerry was a seven-year employee who was promoted to manager of data processing two years ago. Recently a new computer mainframe system had been installed and the applications were undergoing significant rewrites. Jerry was unequaled in his profession. The computer company's representative picked up vibes that Jerry didn't feel appreciated by management. The representative asked for and got an appointment with the company's financial vice president. While there, the sales representative explained and gained concurrence that Jerry was key to the new system implementation. He conveyed that Jerry seemed concerned about something.

Using good call techniques, the representative also discovered that Jerry was significantly underpaid and laid out new insights about pay scales in Jerry's profession. Other issues were also discussed in very businesslike terms. Jerry received a consequential raise and a bonus commitment. The representative enjoyed a positive and ongoing business relationship with the vice president.

You might question whether Jerry ever knew the role played by the computer company representative. You bet! You might wonder if competition ever called on this account. You bet they did! Did they ever get any business there? No, never, not one dollar!

Low Calls

All sales calls are not alike. If you find that yours usually are, then you should know that you have a problem right there. Your low calls should be oriented and directed only to those people associated with the *visible part of the buying cycle.* That's okay, because you should be making all the calls necessary on these people who actually buy or directly influence the buyer.

Sales calls have so many similarities because you and your audience should be discussing your product or service along with the associated terms and conditions. You should know with great certainty where their interests are and the kinds of questions and concerns that are going to surface. They may be equally well-informed about other products that will also fulfill their needs. Your competitors are calling on the same people and are telling their story about how their products can fulfill their needs.

The *user* includes only those people who have personal contact with your product. They touch it every day and make it do whatever it is supposed to do. They will tell you how well it is performing as well as any problems they are having. You'll pick up early warning signals at this level and, if you're not around and they can't tell you, they'll be telling someone else. At this level, your calls are more oriented toward making things work right and less toward selling something. These users don't buy anything, but they can have some influence. Usually, when something works as advertised, they are quiet. When it does not, they can become very vocal. Co-workers, supervisors, and managers do not enjoy unhappy users.

Remember, during this type of call, you are gathering information and presenting yourself as a helpful resource. You are not trying to walk out with a handful of orders that day.

Depending upon the complexity of your product, you may find cases where its application is being compromised by an incompetent user. It is important in such instances that you have cultivated a working relationship with people in charge of the users. You can't let your product fail because of incompetency. Your concerns are not likely to surprise the supervisors and managers.

Managers who oversee several other managers may be described as operational managers. These people sometimes are authorized to buy, or they may decide what is to be purchased and someone else actually signs an order. Basic account coverage will require you to have good contacts at this level because these managers are linked closely to where and how your product is used. They are *implementors,* and they need details. They are tied to the daily business activities and therefore they act a lot like users. You need to let them know that you're there to insure that your products work as they should work.

Your low and high calls will now be more profitable than the calls being made by your competitors. It is sensible to assume that there are other products that can be favorably compared to yours. This is reason enough for you to want to consistently present yours wrapped within a better quality sales call. If you consciously execute the sales process steps from the previous chapter, you will make better calls than you're now making and they will be better than your competitor is making . . . and that's an edge you want.

Middle Management Calls

The next upward targets have a specific title. They are not referred to as department managers, or planning managers, or manager of something. While there are all sorts of variations on this theme, they are likely to be classified as executives—middle management types who may be directors, general managers, and vice presidents. They are not top management, senior management, or company officers. They are, however, at an organizational level where you can achieve most of your account development goals. These people participate in the invisible part of the sales cycle. Therefore, they participate in defining needs necessary to resolve opportunities and problems.

This is where your sales call should be different; not better . . . only different. In Chapter 3, you read about the middle management people who operate at this level. Specifically, middle management runs the businesses on a day-to-day basis. They also find the flaws in the plans developed by senior management. They figure out why things aren't working and usually figure out how to fix them. When they get specific about what is needed, but don't have the resources to make it happen, they can usually go topside, make their case and get what they need . . . if it is available. Their voices are heeded at higher levels and complied with at lower levels. They are excellent call targets, particularly when you want quick decisions.

This chapter has expanded on the idea that your sales calls are the most basic tool that you have—and they can become very powerful. There is no reason that you cannot harness this power and make it work for you every single day.

KEITH'S SOLUTION

Keith's users didn't have any unique allegiance to him, his company, or his product. He viewed them as fickle and ungrateful. Keith seemed to expect something in return for nothing. Perhaps he is under the illusion that when a company buys your products they are also sending a message of confidence and goodwill. They may have bought only out of desperation because of a bad experience with another supplier.

Keith accepted the reality that he must give his users and buyers *reason* to have confidence in him and to appreciate the value and benefits of his products and services. Additionally, he realized that he must set up an account plan designed to *earn* an improved business relationship with old and new contacts in his accounts.

We recognized that his call activity was insufficient and without thoughtful objectives. His calls had not been *special*. Keith reflected on the account development strategies and the advantages of calling high. The sales process clearly could help him make better and more productive calls.

Keith began to make *special sales calls.* They were special because they were preceded by account development goals for each account. They were special because they were made on new customer contacts. And they were special because his messages were customized to the interests and functions of these new contacts. He didn't forget his old contacts with buyers and users. His challenge was to slowly convert "fickle and ungrateful" into respectful and appreciative.

Implementing account development techniques with calls directed at middle managers as well as the users and buyers, Keith was able to show a sincere interest in those who came into contact with his product. In support of this effort, he began to recognize that some users had become innovative in the application of his products, and he found opportunities to compliment them and to make others aware of their creativity. He wrote letters of appreciation and often included new product information.

Keith also began a methodical program of one-on-one training that he classified as a special call situation. He found several situations where the customer could benefit from general information sessions designed to take better advantage of his product's features. Two of these sessions were given to night shift operations . . . who seldom saw any suppliers.

Classifying a particular sales call as *special* has a profound way of causing better preparation and better execution. Initially, it forces the salesperson to ask, "What are my objectives on this call, and how am I going to achieve them?" These questions start the call planning process and will result in more meaningful sales calls.

As emphasized in this chapter, Keith began to carefully select his call targets in each account. He displayed unusual interest in those who used his products and helped them become more adept with its versatility.

The results of sales activities as practiced by the *new* Keith are always the same. Those who can be converted will be converted. Whatever attitudes existed can be changed by making special sales calls that incorporate the techniques and skills discussed throughout this book. And finally, we would direct Keith's attention to Chapters 11 and 12, where he can learn more about the "why and how" of making significant changes in his accounts.

CHAPTER 9

WINNING PRESENTATIONS

A Tough Selling Situation:
Everyone's Sold but Nobody's Buying

Salespeople will always want to avoid anything that slows the selling process. Even so, the reality is that many decisions will have such impact that they need to be sorted out in detail. From the company's point of view, due diligence is a process that leads to better decisions. Committees and task forces may be slow to act, but often they become the only road leading to the sale. It can be a tough sell and is often an open invitation for your competitors to join in the fracas. However, if you can't make something happen outside the committee environment, *you have little choice but to turn to this strategy and do your best. The tough sell described below is representative, but there are also others that will cause you to focus on skillfully orchestrated presentations. One-on-one presentations are key selling situations that position you for the major group presentations. There are no bite-size skills that can give you the success probabilities needed for important presentations. Following the tough selling situation described below, this chapter looks intently at all the presentation dimensions that you need to master to become as professional as you can be.*

YOU

You haven't been able to make the sale. You've tried hard, using all the techniques that you know. It doesn't matter much what your product or service is; you haven't successfully pushed the right buttons with the right people. Throughout the selling process, you have found some who seemed to agree to your suggestions and your proposals, but they didn't seem to want to run anywhere with them. Others listened but seemed apathetic. They all had the ordinary objections, but you handled them well, and they seemed satisfied. You wanted to find a champion willing to push your ideas through the maze, but none has surfaced.

You've considered the personalities involved while making individual calls. You have followed the steps of the Sales Process and you know your calls were getting better. You made a few upper-management calls and got a reasonable hearing at those levels. It didn't surprise you that they referred you to people more closely related to the day-to-day operation. What did surprise you was that these people listened also but seemed unwilling to take a position that could lead to action on your proposals.

This scenario implies that your proposals would affect several different areas of your prospect's business. It is within this framework that decision makers become hard to find. Lacking an obvious problem shared by these different areas, and one of such consequence that it demands a solution, there is no organizational need for anyone to take a power position.

It seems as though you have to help your prospect move into a process within which selected people can all hear the same message simultaneously. Further, and in the presence of each other, there needs to be some concurrence that your proposals have merit. In such a group environment, you would hope for mostly positive reactions, some neutrals, and zero strong dissenters. This would be your first objective.

Your second objective is to cause a decision-making body to be formed from the group. In other words, you need to discover an action body. You are going to try to bring into existence a decision process that the prospect doesn't have in place.

Every planned communication with a customer or prospect must be classified as a presentation. However, the skills and techniques in this section assume that a special, more formal presentation is to be made. A successful Account Development Program will usually include these types of presentations. The more formal presentation may include only one "listener," two, or a group. In any event, the assumption is that the meeting was hard to set up, or that the group isn't going to assemble again. Hence, the presenter must be as good as he or she can be and better also be on target.

Don't give a presentation merely because the opportunity is available to you. Where are you in your Account Development Program? Have you laid a foundation throughout the account that will support a formal presentation objective? Can you achieve the next logical step in your development effort at a lower level or in a less sensitive situation?

GROUP PRESENTATIONS

Presentations to Customer Groups. We don't like group presentations when they are a part of the selling process. Unfortunately, they sometimes become the only avenue available. However, if another route exists; try to take it. There are several reasons for this.

It's difficult to keep group members moving at the same pace. Some always want to push ahead and others want to hang back. There are too many hot buttons, one for each person, and they all want theirs emphasized. It can be extremely tough to stay on schedule and the crowd isn't going to worry about it until someone points out that time is up. You may never get to your key points, which will destroy whatever summary you had in mind. The closing of a group presentation is more difficult to figure out in advance and even harder to pull off. There is merit to the idea that what you can get at the end depends on what happened in the body of the presentation. Since this is much less predictable than in other call situations, it follows that your close may have to be put together on the fly.

You may not be sure who the key people are in the group. They sometimes hang back just to show how democratic they are. Often, the loudest (most vocal) of the group has the least influence but may be using this occasion to climb a notch.

Frequently, your well-charted course for this account can be caused to take off in several directions by a group presentation. After the presentation, you may have to go through a damage control assessment and then take the time (through many calls) to bring your strategy back to its original compass heading.

Sometimes a key person, who has already bought into your proposals, will use you and your presentation to gather the troops and cause them to rally around the changes that he or she plans on making. If you know or sense this, never become too comfortable. People who think of themselves as advisors are seldom so outspoken as when in a group of

near-peers. Dissension is supposed to be permitted; otherwise, why have this kind of meeting. This is where you will
find those who are very keen on a competitive solution . . .
and they will surface in spades. Your competitor may have
converted a member of your audience, and your presentation could become the platform to air your competitor's
strengths. This internal apostle may try to force your presentation into a detailed "feature" comparison. You may be
compelled to become aggressive in such situations, or you'll
forfeit both control and direction. Experience suggests that
the competitive disciple appears about 50 percent of the
time.

These presentations are fertile grounds for those who
don't get enough chances to impress the boss . . . and even
their peers. The ranking manager may allow and even enjoy
such actions. The bad news is that protocol for such meetings (in this case, your presentation) have already been established. They have lots of meetings like this and they
know what they can get away with. They know the rules,
but you may not. If the troops won't rally, you may lose the
high cards that you already had.

Groups don't make decisions unless they are specifically
chartered to do so. Chartered groups (committees and task
forces) usually are expected to study possible courses of action and make recommendations. Since most groups don't
make decisions but only influence them, one certainly has
reason to ask, "Why am I planning to do this?" This is a
pertinent question and you must have the right answer before you promote or even agree to a presentation.

If you still feel that a presentation is the next best step for
your strategy, then we suggest that you carefully orchestrate
the customer's objectives and expectations about the presentation. Having done this, insure that every attendee understands what the mission is and what it is not. It should be
clear by now that while presentations have a place in your
selling, they may also leave you vulnerable in several consequential ways. In this regard, your audience should understand that you're there to tell them something. It could be a

technology update. It could be anything . . . but it is a presentation and not an open two-way street. Their expectations will have much to do with the role that they play.

And finally, *you will have to make presentations.* Group presentation situations are different and demand your special attention. The following information will help you move your group presentations from average to very good. We have provided a summary in outline form that can be found in the Appendix. Use it for review and as a final checklist before every presentation.

PRE-PRESENTATION LOGISTICS

Set the Stage. Stage setting is important for any presentation, but it is particularly important for presentations to groups. The more carefully you prepare your presentation and the stage from which you will present it, the more likely you are to succeed.

Your Place or Theirs? This very basic decision deserves careful thought. There are advantages and disadvantages at both locations. Some advantages of giving a presentation at your place are as follows:

1. There are no interruptions. If you go to their place, you may have to contend with a variety of interruptions.

2. You gain some psychological dominance because it is your territory.

3. Your equipment will probably work better. This is particularly important if you need visual aids or machinery for your presentation.

4. Prospects can meet your management. This can add appeal to your presentation because most people like to meet upper management types.

5. You can impress them with the solidity and strength of your organization. If you own your building or have fancy offices, it can increase prospects' confidence in your organization.

6. You have key information sources available in your organization. If a problem arises, you can call on the experts. They are also useful for providing answers to highly technical questions that you would rather not discuss while the senior people are present. You can send their specialist off to talk to your specialist, or say that you will set up a meeting right after the presentation.

7. You can give a longer presentation and be reasonably sure you will get the time that you request. People will generally not travel for a 15- or 20-minute presentation, but they might insist on that time limit if you meet at their offices. They might also insist that you shorten your presentation at the last minute because some crisis has arisen.

8. It is an automatic qualifier; people are expressing interest by making the commitment to come to your place.

9. It can take a great deal of time to set up a meeting at their place. People may not do the things they promised to do; rooms aren't ready, lights don't work, projectors don't operate or aren't available, and you must check everything personally.

There are also many advantages to making your presentation at their place:

1. Your audience will probably feel more comfortable. Remember, your goal is to make them comfortable and receptive to your presentation. Most people feel more comfortable in their own territory; although, a few prefer to get away from their offices so they can give you their undivided attention.

2. They will be more willing to attend a presentation at their place than at yours. It takes less time, less trouble, and so on. Asking them to come to your place may even reduce your chances of making the presentation and getting the commitments.

3. It is usually easier to understand them in their own building. They are more comfortable and relaxed. Observing where people sit, how they relate to each other, and who comes on time to the meeting can provide you with helpful information about the decision makers.

4. If you need the approval of someone who is not at the meeting, it may be possible to get it immediately afterward while the momentum is in your favor. This is important. If it takes too long to get the next level of approval, you may lose the decision.

5. Presenting at their place forces you to plan more carefully. You must decide exactly what you're going to do because your equipment and personnel support are limited. These limitations can reduce the natural laziness that your own territory can create.

6. If someone from the audience's organization helps you with the arrangements, you can learn a great deal. Secretaries and administrative assistants are an invaluable source of information.

The Invitation. Before your presentation, send an invitation to every invited attendee. The invitation should include the following:

1. The Place and Time of the Presentation. If you aren't certain that people know how to find the place, give detailed instructions or a map.

2. List of Attendees. Indicate who is expected to attend. At the end of your list write: "If your understanding is

different from mine, please contact me." That simple sentence can prevent some unpleasant surprises.

3. List of Your Main Points. List the points you will cover. Then ask if there are any additional subjects they would like to discuss. This can help you learn what your audience wants you to talk about.

The invitation should be brief enough to be read in a minute or two. If properly done, the invitation can prevent many problems that frequently occur. For example; people not knowing when or where the presentation is, high ranking executives arriving unexpectedly, important topics omitted, etc.

The Preparation Visit. If you give your presentation at their place, you should visit the location at least one day in advance. Make sure the room is large enough, well ventilated, and otherwise suited for your purpose. If the room seems inadequate, try to change it.

Check out each piece of equipment. Don't leave that for the last minute. You may be unable to locate the tape recorder or overhead projector, or they may not work. It is, of course, safer to bring your own equipment, but that can offend some people.

If possible, ask for a secretary or an administrative assistant to help you with your arrangements. You will find equipment, conference rooms and whatever else you need more quickly, and you will also learn a good deal about the organization. For example, you may find that people arrive later than you expected or take lunch at a different time than you normally do. If you planned your presentation for 8:30 and you discover that people don't normally arrive before 8:45, change your starting time. As you work together setting things up, ask about internal customs.

You can also learn about people's attitudes toward presentations. How long do they like presentations to be? What kind of language do they prefer? How would they like to sit?

How do they like to handle coffee breaks? These insights can help you achieve your goal.

Equipment and Visual Aids. Every piece of equipment should be checked carefully no more than one day before your presentation. Make sure you have spares for parts that break down easily. If your equipment fails, your entire presentation can fall apart.

Have someone else look at your visual aids with a fresh pair of eyes. Do they seem effective? Do they hit hard? Do they make exactly the points you want them to make?

When you set up the room, make sure your visual aids are covered. If the audience sees them too soon, your words can compete with your visual aids. Attendees may be looking at them while you are talking about something else. Furthermore, if people see them too soon, the visual aids lose their dramatic impact. You want your audience to look at them at exactly the right moment.

PRESENTATION TIME HAS ARRIVED

Seating Arrangements. Many presenters leave this to chance, but you will experience more success if you control these arrangements, particularly for large groups. Put name cards where you want people to sit; most people will automatically follow these directions.

Controlling the seating arrangements subtly communicates: "I'm in charge." It prevents forgetting people's names and milling around at the start of the meeting, and it puts the decision makers where you want them. They should be as close to you as possible so you can relate to them personally and show them all of your visual aids, models, and other materials.

If possible, put yourself between the audience and the door. This will reduce the number of people who slip out quietly during your presentation. It also reduces interruptions from secretaries and other people. When they realize they must walk past you to give a message to someone, they may decide to wait until the presentation is over.

Socializing Before the Presentation. The larger the group, the longer the delay between the arrival of the first and the last person. This period can be uncomfortable for everyone, but it is also an opportunity to establish a psychological link with your audience. You can meet each of them individually.

Shake hands with everyone and try to build rapport. Look for each person's reactions. See which ones seem most interested and which ones seem skeptical or hostile about even being there. (Some were told to come.)

Look for signs about the general atmosphere. Does the group seem interested, bored, enthusiastic? Do they defer to one or two people? Does there seem to be cliques or hostility among groups? In other words, use the time before the presentation to create a relationship and to learn as much as you can about your audience. Then adjust your presentation to fit the situation.

Sell the Decision Makers. Before the presentation, decide whose approval you need to achieve your objective, then concentrate on selling them. Who are the real decision makers? If many people have nearly equal power, divide the audience into three categories: those who have already agreed, those who will never agree, and those you have to convince. Ignore both extreme types. Concentrate on the swing votes, the people who have not yet made up their minds.

Once you have decided who your targets are, select the kind of presentation that will most appeal to them. What length, arguments, and amount of detail will they prefer? As you present, observe their reactions and adjust your presentation to maximize its appeal to these critically important people.

Important decisions are seldom made during group presentations; they are made afterward by the decision makers.

Before your presentation begins, arrange to meet with them immediately after the presentation. You will lose momentum if you don't have these meetings immediately. Other people will make suggestions, new problems will demand attention and some of your points will be forgotten. The group presentation creates momentum toward action; capitalize on it in an immediate meeting with the decision makers.

Relate to Everyone. Although you concentrate on a few decision makers, make sure you relate to your entire audience. Move your eyes from person to person. Address some of your remarks to various individuals. If possible, make direct name references to each member of the audience. In other words, don't make anyone feel excluded; they may become insulted and work actively against you.

Tighten Your Organization. The larger your audience becomes, the tighter your organization must be. With one person you can correct organizational errors through a discussion. However, with a loose organization in a group presentation, you may lose control or confuse your audience. Use more visual aids and make them simple and clear. Pictures speak a common language that both technical and nontechnical people can understand.

Communicate Authority. The larger the group, the more important your authority becomes. If your manner does not demand respect and attention, you will lose your audience. A few techniques will increase your authority in presentations to groups.

1. Stand up. Looking down at people gives you control.

2. Stand close to your audience. The closer you are, the more they must look up to you. This increases the psychological impact of the standing position.

3. Speak in a resonant, clear voice. Show them you're proud of what you have to say.

4. Use authoritative, confident gestures. Your voice and your manner should clearly communicate: "I'm in charge."

5. Keep it short. Group presentations should be shorter than those to individuals. Since there is less exchange, the audience will get restless faster.

6. Answer questions confidently. Never appear frightened or flustered. If you do not have the answer, say in a confident way: "I don't have the answer right now, but I will get it for you when the meeting is over."

7. Do not let people challenge or undermine your authority. People will often try to prove you are wrong, show they are smarter than you, or make speeches to your audience. Don't let them get away with it. Don't attack or insult them, but make sure you stay in command. If you encounter a hostile or argumentative question, say you will answer it after the meeting. If someone tries to make a speech, say you think that level of detail is inappropriate now and you would be happy to discuss it privately. Don't be afraid that your audience won't like it when you resist challenges to your authority; nearly everyone wants and expects you to maintain control of your presentation.

Summary. When presenting to groups, your critical problem is to maintain control without becoming rigid, cold or authoritarian. Most of these recommendations are oriented toward increasing your control. The tighter your organization, the more control you will have. Concentrating on one or a few decision makers keeps your presentation on track. Stage setting creates an environment and mood that support your authority. An authoritative manner captures the audience's attention, builds their confidence in you and reduces interruptions and distractions.

PRESENTATION SALES SKILLS

There are basic selling skills that are equally applicable whether you are presenting to several people or to a larger group in a formal setting. Therefore, working on these skills results in better presentations at all levels. However, as group size increases, your techniques are modified to capture the diversity inherent in group situations.

Each presentation can be divided into two distinct segments: (1) *content and organization*—the words you say; (2) *delivery techniques and sensitivity*—the way you speak and relate to your listeners. These topics are logically distinct and should be kept separate during your preparation.

Content and Organization

While preparing the presentation, spend as much time as it takes to clearly define your presentation objectives and decide how you're going to convey these to your audience. Know exactly what it is you're going to ask for. Build your presentation in a backward fashion, moving from close, to summary, then to body, and finally on to the planned opening. (Your summary may be incomplete until your body segment is firm.)

As you begin the process, consciously remember that the only purpose of a presentation is to create desire for your recommendation. Convincing people that it is logical to agree with you is not enough. They may agree but not take action. You must try to create desire that is strong enough to overcome their reluctance to make commitments.

Set a Clear Objective. Your objective is what you want people to do after you make your presentation. Unfortunately, many presenters do not have a clear objective. They focus on what they will do or say, not on what they want their audience to do.

Obviously you want some form of commitment. Exactly what is the commitment? Do you want an agreement signed today? Do you need approval for something that will be signed by the Purchasing Department or another unit? Do you want the decision maker to act as your internal salesperson? Be specific about what you want the audience to do; then make sure every word supports your objective.

Structure your presentation so that it provides a logical path toward your objective. A presentation is not a random collection of ideas and recommendations. It must be clearly structured to cover all your points in the right order. The four major parts of each presentation—the opening, body, summary, and close—are covered here in the sequence that your audience will hear them.

The Opening. The opening is the place to provide an overview of your entire presentation. Your listener(s) should know where you are going by the end of the first minute. A visual overview aid is extremely helpful. Even if you tell people that you will discuss four points, most of them cannot remember all four or how they fit together. When the points are written, listeners feel more comfortable and learn more from your presentation. It takes only a few seconds to make that opening statement, and the visual aids are simple and inexpensive to prepare.

The Body. The body provides the details. You might discuss the specifics of the example and relate them to opportunities. Large chunks of your company's "story" might be the supporting framework of the body of the presentation.

The body should be carefully organized so that each major point is discussed. The most important points should come first and last. People remember those points better than points made in the middle. As you move from one point to the next, tell your listeners. If you don't make clear transitions, they may get lost. A transition for the presentation might be, "We have seen how this approach can expand your options. Now let's look at the financial implications."

The Summary. The summary pulls things together and helps the listener to understand the relationship between your major points. It also prepares the listener psychologically for your close.

The Close. It is your punch line. Your presentation should create a desire to act. Exploit that desire by asking for the commitment. If they are surprised by your close, then it follows that you really fouled up the body and the summary!

Link Everything to the Audience's Problems or Goals.
Show exactly how your recommendation meets their requirement. If you made your diagnosis at a previous meeting, start with a brief summary of the results. Make sure they agree with your analysis; if not, change it. Then say that you will show exactly how your recommendation addresses their situation. Each time you introduce a new subject, relate it directly to their requirements.

The audience is considering other possible solutions, so you must show how your recommendation is superior—not in a general sense, but as a solution to their particular problems. Many presenters ignore competition. They talk only about their solution, leaving the comparison process to the audience. If the audience makes the comparisons, it will be less favorable to you than if you make it. You should state exactly how your recommendation does a better job of solving their problems. Make sure that you do not appear to be "knocking" the competition; that will offend some people.

If you directly link your recommendation to the listeners' problems or goals and show how it is superior to the competition, their job becomes easier. They understand why they should commit to you. They also have more confidence in you. They recognize that you aren't just making a canned presentation or "letting the recommendation speak for itself." You are working with them to achieve their objectives.

Emphasize Benefits, Not Features. People are much less interested in your recommendation than in what it can do for them. They care about its benefits, not its features. Unfortunately, most presentations emphasize features, not benefits. Presenters generally know much more about their solution than they do about their audience's requirements. It is easy to talk about 350 horsepower, or 100 percent polyester. But people are much less interested in these features than they are in safety while passing or smaller dry-cleaning bills. You are always more effective when you're talking about benefits. It is only in this way that your audience knows what your solution can do for them.

Keep It Short and Simple. You can be specific and concrete without telling long stories or going into excessive detail. Details bore and confuse listeners. Many presenters go into detail or tell long stories because they are afraid listeners will not understand their points. But your goal is not to tell all that you know; it is to walk out with a commitment. The shorter and simpler your presentation is, the better your chances.

Listeners never get angry if a presentation is shorter than they anticipated, but if you talk too long, many of them will lose interest. You may believe you have to cover every point, but most people just want the highlights. Don't be afraid that you won't say enough. Listeners will ask for any information they want, and they prefer a give-and-take exchange to an interminable monologue. Set a time limit for your presentations; then cut it by one-third, and make sure you stay on your schedule.

Avoid Jargon. Nearly all listeners are irritated and confused by jargon. You may think that using the "buzz words" of your field proves your knowledge and sophistication, but it just frustrates most people. Part of relating to people on their terms is speaking a language they understand and enjoy using. Unless they have used your jargon themselves, use simple, common language.

Close Strategy. Your close should be strong and memorable. Your entire presentation should build toward the close in the same way a good play builds toward the final curtain. Then, when their desire is greatest, ask for the commitment in the strongest and most impressive way.

Depend on Basic Selling Skills

Don't Tell; Sell. Don't talk about your solution, sell it. Make sure every word contributes toward getting that commitment. If they know what you're going for, it's all the better. Concentrate on arousing the listener's desire. Your presentation should create enough desire to get action. The following principles will help you stimulate desire.

Appeal to Emotions. Most decisions are influenced by emotions. Try to discover your listener's emotions, then appeal to them in your presentation. For example, people buy smoke detectors out of fear of fire. A good presentation can arouse that fear, then show that, with the smoke detector, fear can be changed to a logical and preplanned course of action. (The feature is detection and alarm. The benefit is that they get to live).

Tell Stories That Illustrate Your Main Points. Abstractions and statistics do not move most people. Stories, pictures, and examples have much more impact. For example, a good sales presentation for smoke detectors would not cite lots of statistics. It would make prospects smell smoke, see flames and hear children screaming. "Roots" had a much greater impact on most people than an endless historical analysis of slavery and discrimination could have had. You can do the same thing. Tell stories, create word pictures, and provide examples that people can relate to intellectually *and* emotionally. Support your main points by using the E3 formula. Quote *E*xperts, provide crisp *E*vidence and use pertinent *E*xamples.

Use Visual Aids. One picture is worth a thousand words. Visual aids (pictures, models, graphics) can express many points you just cannot explain in words. They can also arouse emotions better than words.

Summary. The only purpose of the presentation is to create a desire to act. You must say the right words in the right way. When you plan your presentations, set a clear objective. Decide exactly what you want the audience to do; then make every word consistent with that objective. *Structure your presentation so that the opening provides an overview, the body discusses the details, the summary pulls things together and clarifies the relationship between the main points, and the close exploits desire by asking for a commitment.*

Link everything to the audience's problems or goals. Show exactly why your recommendation is their answer. Emphasize the benefits, not features. Tell people what your solution will do for them. Avoid details and jargon. Keep it short and simple. Close strongly. Make your entire presentation build toward that close; then be sure you ask for the commitment in the strongest, most memorable way. In other words, don't talk about your recommendation, SELL IT!

LINKING WITH YOUR AUDIENCE

Words alone rarely get results. Your manner, delivery and sensitivity to people have as much impact as your words. Your words should link your solution to the listener's situation. Your manner will link (or unlink) you to people. You need both types of links. Audiences obviously want solutions, but they also want you to relate to them as human beings.

The following will tell you how to deliver presentations that link you to your listener. It covers two general topics: (1) Delivery—the general methods for creating a favorable image of yourself and your solution; and (2) *Sensitivity*—techniques for adjusting to personalities, moods, situations, and the impact of your own personality.

Delivery Techniques

Your delivery greatly affects an audience's reaction to your presentation. A poor delivery can ruin the impact of excellent words, while an excellent delivery can make "the sale" even when your words are weak. Of course, the best combination is a good delivery of a well-organized presentation. Your delivery must express confidence in yourself and your message. The more confident you appear, the more confident and receptive your audience will become. The **"Self/Message/Audience Scale"** is an index of your self confidence and ability to relate effectively to your audience.

Self			Message			Audience		
1	2	3	4	5	6	7	8	9

Self—1, 2, 3. In this category you have hardly any confidence. You concentrate on yourself and worry about what people think of you. Are my clothes all right? Am I standing straight? Do they think I'm prepared? Of course, the more you worry about their impression of you, the worse impression you create. . . . So Look Good!

Message—4, 5, 6. In this category you're somewhat more confident. You focus on the ideas you want to communicate. You try to make sure your words and visual aids are right. Unfortunately, you're so concerned with the content and organization of your presentation that you don't create that essential link to the audience. . . . So Sound Good!

Audience—7, 8, 9. In this category you have confidence in yourself and your message. You're so sure of your presentation that you concentrate on relating personally to people. . . . So Be Good!

The ideal rating floats between 6 and 7. You should forget yourself and think about both your message and your audience. You cannot do that until you gain confidence in yourself and your message. If you're not used to making presentations, you will worry about your image and your message. If you have not *planned and rehearsed* your presentation carefully, you will worry about your message. But if you're sure of yourself and your message, you can split your attention between message and audience, and that helps achieve the results that you're looking for.

Command Their Respect. To accomplish anything, you must command audience respect. Your manner should communicate that you expect them to listen carefully because you deserve an attentive audience. You can tell them that meetings that consume time and talent must achieve a specific purpose and that you respect that position.

Project Enthusiasm. If you act like you believe in what you're saying, listeners are more likely to believe it too. Let them know: "I'm glad to be here. I've got something important to tell you." Never apologize by saying something like: "I'm sorry to take your time." You are not taking their time. You're giving them answers to important questions.

Maintain Eye Contact. When you are looking at your audience, they feel you're relating to them. Don't challenge them with your eyes or stare at them too intently. Just look comfortably at them most of the time.

Demand Their Attention. If they aren't paying attention, wait confidently and quietly until they do. Don't try to talk while they are reading, looking at visual aids, answering the telephone, or are otherwise diverted. Wait, and make them come back to you. They will.

Control Your Gestures. Your gestures should support your authority. Stand erect, use your hands forcefully, and avoid any hint of insecurity. Don't fold your arms, wring your hands, scratch yourself, stand rigidly, or move around nervously. Let your body show that you are comfortable and confident because you know you can help them.

Be Proud of Your Costs. Never be apologetic about your costs; that tells people you don't think your solution is really worth its cost. Don't avoid discussing your costs or be hesitant when you talk about them. Mention cost in a calm, comfortable manner that says you believe it is fully justified. On the other hand, do not oversell the costs. People will wonder why you feel obliged to argue so forcefully.

Don't Lecture. Speak to your listeners, not at them. Authority is essential, but arrogance is intolerable. Let your listeners know that your expertise is being made available to them. You're working with them to achieve their goals.

Punctuate With Your Voice. Oral presentations are much harder to understand than written ones. A reader can refer to an earlier point or reread a passage, but a listener does not have these options. Furthermore, written sentences are much better structured than spoken ones. If you doubt that, tape a presentation and have parts of it transcribed. When you look at your sentences in print, you may not believe you said them. Many will be much too long, and some of them will not be sentences at all. You may change subjects in the middle of sentences, have sentences that wander off and end nowhere, and so on. As you read the transcript, you will see how hard it is to follow your own thoughts.

It is even more difficult for a listener to follow your thoughts. So make things easy for your audience. Add punctuation marks with your voice. A very short pause equals a comma. A longer one represents a period. A still longer one is equal to a break between paragraphs. Lift your voice at the end of questions. Speak more loudly to underline your main points. This punctuation will keep listeners interested and help them to understand and follow your thoughts.

Practice Your Presentation. Without practice, your presentation will not flow smoothly. You cannot expect to deliver a professional presentation without practicing it at least twice. Make sure you know all the points you will make, the order in which you will make them, and the examples and other evidence you will use to support them. Do not memorize your presentation. If it sounds memorized, it will lack spontaneity and forcefulness. Listeners want to feel that you are relating to them. Use cue scripts, outline notes and visual aids to keep you on the track, but practice until you don't need these aids constantly.

No matter how much you practice; you will occasionally forget a point. Just ignore it and keep moving. Remembering it will probably not make much difference, but your audience will lose confidence in you if you stand there wondering: "Where was I?"

Encourage Dialogue. Sometimes a formal presentation is appropriate, but it is usually better to involve listeners in a controlled discussion. Encourage questions and comments and respond positively to them. Pause from time to time. Ask for reactions and be sensitive to nonverbal messages. If listeners seem confused, dubious or annoyed, find out why; then change your emphasis, language, tone, or pace.

Sensitivity

It is not enough to deliver a well-organized presentation in a confident, natural way. You have to also adjust to each listener's personality, mood and situation, as well as to the natural impact of your own personality.

Adjust to Listeners' Personalities. You should know your listeners' personality types. Your understanding should be more sophisticated than our simple classification of *dominant, detached and relational* types (Chapter 4). Therefore, you should modify the following recommendations to allow for the other characteristics you have observed.

Dominant Listeners. They tend to be impatient, and they do not enjoy listening to long presentations. Be brief, well organized, and avoid details. Never stretch the truth with them. Exaggerations will increase their natural skepticism. Exaggerations also give them a chance to attack you, and they may do so just to challenge you. Do not try to anticipate and respond to every possible objection. That would make your presentation too long. When answering objections, encourage a dialogue. When they are just listening, you're in control, which makes them uncomfortable. Dominant listeners will participate actively in most presentations.

It is extremely important that you maintain your authority. They may interrupt frequently with objections or questions. Don't fight the interruptions or evade their point, but firmly control the presentation. If you lose control, they lose confidence in you.

Detached Listeners. They enjoy listening, like details, and want evidence to support your points. Your presentation should be detailed, impersonal, factual, and slightly longer than presentations to the other two personality types. To satisfy their need for details and supporting evidence, prepare handouts before the presentation. Put the bulk of the details and evidence in the handouts and check them for accuracy. Detached people read material very carefully and are intolerant of errors. They are likely to ask questions about the handouts, so make sure you understand every point in them. If they quiz you on a minor point, and you don't respond satisfactorily, you can destroy your credibility.

Relational Listeners. They respond very well to authority when it is combined with warmth and personal concern for them. Show your concern in an authoritative but not particularly forceful manner. Talk about people, their concerns and activities. Keep control, but encourage a dialogue. If they digress, gently bring them back on the track.

Adjust to Listeners' Moods. Continually look for signs of interest, acceptance, agreement, boredom, impatience, confusion, or hostility. When you see them, adjust your presentation.

Interest. People show their interest by leaning forward, maintaining eye contact, nodding their heads, taking notes, studying visual aids and samples, and asking questions. Look for these signs of interest, especially during your opening statement. Which points seem most interesting and important to them? Which ones seem irrelevant? If it seems necessary, change your emphasis, pace, or even your main points.

Agreement and Disagreement. If a listener disagrees with one of your points, the sooner you adjust to it the better. It is particularly important to check for agreement while you're summarizing the audience's requirements. Agreement signs are similar to those of interest but also include words such as: "That's right," "Okay" or "I agree." If people disagree with your summary, correct it immediately; then adjust your presentation.

Boredom and Impatience. You cannot afford to bore your audience. Even if they need exactly what you propose, a boring presentation can cost you a commitment. Signs of boredom include doodling, fidgeting, tapping fingers or a pencil on the furniture, looking at something else, and comments such as: "That's obvious."

If your analysis of their situation is correct, but your listeners act impatient or bored, you're probably talking too generally. You may be discussing your solution or organization, and they would rather discuss their specific needs. Whatever the cause, whenever you see signs of boredom or impatience, react. Drop the subject as quickly and gracefully as you can and move to subjects that interest your audience. If listeners seem bored by the entire presentation, you may be moving too slowly. Drop some of your points, compress other ones and encourage a discussion. Most people would rather talk than listen. An exchange will increase their interest, and their comments will help you to redirect your presentation.

Confusion. If listeners are confused, they are not going to commit. Although some signs are obvious, many people are embarrassed to admit or show their confusion. So try to be sensitive to their subtle messages. Blank looks are easy to notice, but many of them occur for only an instant. Repeated questions or requests for additional information often suggest confusion.

If you sense any confusion, do not ask, "Are you confused?" or say, "This is hard to understand." People could feel that you're criticizing their intelligence. Suggest that you may not have communicated clearly. You might say: "I don't think I have expressed myself very clearly on that point. Let me come at it a different way." If the listener agrees, go for it. If not, continue with your original outline, but use simpler language and cite more examples.

Skepticism. Most people are skeptical. They know presenters tend to exaggerate and present their recommendations in the most favorable way. Some skepticism is natural, so ignore it. If you see signs of considerable skepticism, probe gently. What doubts do they have? What causes these doubts? Then relieve the doubts with objective evidence, testimonials or references to people who already agree with your analysis.

Hostility. Hostility is communicated by clenched fists or teeth, averted eye contact, pointing a finger or pencil at you, a loud voice, a red face, and in many other ways. Your natural reaction to hostility may be anger. However, you cannot afford to become angry. When you detect signs of hostility, probe gently for the underlying reasons. What have you said or done that was offensive? Apologize or correct the false impression, then ask for permission to continue. These steps often relieve tension and give you a chance to make your points.

No Reaction. The low reactor is the most difficult person to convince. You want reactions, both to gain the commitment and to make yourself more comfortable. Low reactors make some presenters so uncomfortable that they tend to talk too much, too fast, and too loudly, and a few people will even exaggerate or lie. When you encounter a low reactor, make a short, factual presentation and close. Try to force them to respond to your request for action; their responses will help you plan your next moves.

Time Pressure. Before beginning your presentation, find out how much time people can spend with you. If it is less than you had anticipated, ask if it is possible to take a little longer. If they are reluctant to grant additional time, shorten your presentation. If necessary, reschedule it. Make sure you don't run over the time limit. If listeners are irritated and cannot wait for you to finish, you have no chance for a commitment. Short presentations to receptive listeners produce more action than longer presentations to irritated and preoccupied audiences.

Competition. When competitors are meeting with the same group, try to make the last presentation. You can usually learn from audience reactions how your proposal compares to those of the competition. Then, if necessary, you can adjust your presentations. You can also directly compare your solution and the competitors' on those points that are most important to the listeners. If you are unable to go last, try to arrange a second meeting after all your competitors have made their presentations. You can then answer any objections and make those important comparisons.

Interruptions. Accept interruptions as gracefully as possible. You cannot afford to show annoyance. After each interruption, backtrack a little in your presentation to make sure your audience is with you. Make certain you have their full attention before beginning again. If they are distracted, offer to delay your presentation until they resolve their new problems. Most listeners will then realize you want their full attention and will try to give it to you. If they cannot do so, wait a few moments while they resolve their problems, or reschedule the presentation for a later date.

Distractions. Interruptions are only one form of distraction. In an office, people may be walking back and forth, telephones may be ringing at other desks, and loud machinery may be running. The best way to deal with distractions is to eliminate them. Where possible, make your presentations in a quiet place. If you cannot do so, try to make the distractions less disruptive. If noise is the problem, raise your voice and speak slowly and clearly. Use more visual aids to hold the listener's interest. Shorten your presentation and have more of a conversation because distractions shorten a listener's attention span. Above all, do not show irritation. The distractions may bother you intensely, but the more irritated you appear the less receptive people will become.

Adjust to Your Natural Impact. You should have a good understanding of the type of presenter you are. During the presentation, continually assess your impact on other people, then adjust to it. Build on your natural strengths and compensate for your weaknesses.

Dominant Presenters. If you are dominant, your presentations are probably short, well-organized, and hard-hitting. You generally appear authoritative, confident, and enthusiastic. Build on those strengths.

However, you may also tend to diagnose problems superficially. If you do, your presentations may not relate directly to listeners' problems and interest. You may also be moderately insensitive to the messages listeners send you during the presentation. Be more sensitive to their moods. Look especially for signs that they feel you're pushing too hard. In other words, if you are dominant, use your natural authority; but try not to be overbearing or insensitive.

Detached Presenters. If you are detached, your presentations are probably logical and well-organized. You also provide convincing evidence to support your recommendations. However, your presentations may lack emotional appeal, and they are probably too long. You may try to present the complete picture, including all the minor facts. Your presentations may sound like professorial lectures rather than action-oriented presentations.

Build on your ability to diagnose thoroughly and organize your thoughts, but shorten your presentation and appeal to emotions. Replace facts and statistics with stories and examples. When you deliver the presentation, project more warmth and forcefulness. Maintain eye contact and use strong, confident gestures.

Relational Presenters. If you are relational, you relate well to people and are quite sensitive to the messages they send you. In fact, you may be too sensitive. You may be so concerned with reactions that your presentations lack force and movement. For example, there may be so much debate that your presentations become wandering conversations rather than organized attempts to create desire. You may even omit important topics because you're afraid they will offend, annoy, or bore the audience. Build on your ability to create a strong bond with listeners, but make sure your presentations are forceful, organized and authoritative.

SUMMARY

Good words are not enough. Well-organized presentations link your solutions to people's problems, but you also need a personal link between yourself and the audience. Your delivery techniques and sensitivity provide that link.

Command their attention with a confident manner, enthusiasm, strong gestures, and frequent eye contact. Help your audience follow your presentations with pauses and other "punctuation marks." Practice until you can deliver your presentation smoothly and naturally. Encourage dialogue. Audiences will become more involved, which will help you to adjust to their personalities, moods, and circumstances.

Finally, adjust to the impact of your own personality. If you are dominant, exploit your natural authority, but do not overwhelm listeners. If you are detached, build on your diagnostic and organizational strengths but shorten your presentations, appeal to emotions, and show warmth. If you are relational, use your warmth and sensitivity but make sure your presentations are forceful and well-organized.

YOUR SOLUTION

When prospective customers are listening but none of them have stepped forward to take charge, the solution lies in creating a core consensus that your proposal has merit and should be seriously considered.

Faced with these circumstances, your best hope is to keep your sale alive and create a decision-making body. There must be an agreed upon charter that this "body" is supposed to go away and do something.

Even after your presentation is over, there is much work to be done. What has been achieved thus far is that you now have people to sell to.

Presentations are a risky environment. If done poorly, they can be a disaster. Selection of attendees will have much to do with how this meeting progresses. The presentation requires careful preparation and precise orchestration. Following the steps for making good presentations will give you another powerful selling tool.

The tough selling situation described at the beginning of this chapter will be encountered in most of your Account Development efforts. Other situations, kissing cousins to this one, may also call for a formal group presentation. A professional salesperson should anticipate and plan for such presentations so that they may become his or her stock in trade.

Our note of sincere caution is that a poorly executed presentation is likely to be devastating. It can wipe out most of what you have previously done in an account. There is honestly no excuse for this happening.

CHAPTER 10

NEGOTIATE, ACCOMMODATE, COMPROMISE

A Tough Selling Situation:

Selling Around Imposed Constraints

The most basic understanding that a salesperson must grasp is that customers will buy to meet the needs of their company. Your product is offered into the marketplace to satisfy these needs wherever possible. Both buyer and seller have learned that perfect matches are seldom possible and seek to narrow the gap through negotiation, accommodation, and compromise. Information and sensitivity will be the seller's most rewarding companions as the selling process unfolds.

MATT

This week, it seemed to Matt that he had been doing more arguing than selling. He had won some points and he had lost some. The losses had been discouraging. On the one hand, he was fending off customers' demands, while on the other he was trying to get his own company to show more flexibility toward satisfying customers' requirements. He could identify with being the messenger whom no one wanted to hear.

During the week, Matt had faced the complex "procurement process" at Kenyann Enterprises and received a formal Request for Information from National Regulator. Attached to the request was a product specification sheet with 23 questions requiring a narrative response. Matt could name seven other companies that were also probably looking at the same request.

Included in this week's impasses had been his company's un-yielding position on shipment quantities and frequency along with a flat refusal to post a performance bond. From the customers' and prospects' side had come a request for extended terms and a re-fusal to accept the limits of a liability clause as presented in Matt's Sales Contract. It had not been a fruitful week!

Negotiation, accommodation, and compromise occur every day in the business arena. The frequency and degree, how-ever, depend upon the nature of the business. Tradition and customary practices and attitudes seem to stimulate a need to negotiate—a common practice in the building trades, for example.

In the world of business-to-business selling, negotiation can be present, but most sellers and some buyers understand that the practice has very real limitations. Even so, many customers will work hard to include the practice in the buy-ing process. This leaves the salesperson with a problem. He or she is sandwiched in the middle (accommodation), and on either side lie negotiation and compromise like forbidden ground. It follows that accommodation has to be used strategically to reduce dependency upon either of the two extremes. Even so, if you have little or no room to negotiate or compromise (because of your company's constraints), you have to *appear* to be doing them. It's a good trick, and a game you may have to play. You will win at this game by anticipating, reading the offense, and setting up a defense that keeps the buyer a little confused.

Most people immediately think of negotiation, accommodation, and compromise as having something to do with prices or costs. They may, but the typical salesperson has almost no actual room to move on either price or cost. Certainly, he or she can't control cost. If it's a manufactured product, it includes raw materials, tooling, machining, labor, and so on. Then there are packaging costs plus shipping or transportation. There are distribution costs, and all along the way there are general and administrative costs . . . and, of course, there is a profit requirement for your company to stay in business. After these are all added up, they are translated into a firm price.

Many people want to equate *negotiating* with *bargaining* and make the latter a part of their buying process. To some extent, it has always been that way. Remember, however, that a bargain is something bought cheaply or advantageously. It's a settlement sometimes thought of as coming to terms. A common feeling is that if one party got a bargain, then the other didn't. The aftertaste of a bargain is the feeling that, had you been more persistent, you could have gotten a better deal. In a subsequent transaction with the same buyer, you can expect that the last bargain has now become the standard and the starting place for today's negotiations. The act of bargaining can also degenerate into haggling. None of us want to be there.

Accommodation is a real step up in the process of selling and buying. It is here that we try to oblige, adapt, and adjust within those boundaries that are tolerable to both the buyers and sellers. *Compromise* is some sort of understanding that may or may not involve concessions. It usually consists of movement by both parties or sides.

We all negotiate, accommodate, and compromise every day, in all walks of life. When you say, "I'll give you that point," you have elected to move off your spot to give yourself, or the other party, an opportunity to go forward. "Yes, I do understand and appreciate that" has about the same effect.

When selling, we can allow the other person(s) to win everything except the one thing for which we are there. We want to condition them for the big fall. When we get good at selling, we can give points along the way, while simultaneously firming up our primary case. The points you choose to give away must seem to have some value to the buyer, but in reality, they are of little or no cost to you. Giving points away in this manner is very serious business because if they appear to be free, then by definition the buyer cannot place much value upon them and will be unable to demonstrate appreciation for them.

If the customer wants all 10,000 units within 30 days, but your normal terms are that you'll ship within 60 days, you can build a case (and take points) while planning on your technique of giving them back. You'll explain that executing such a commitment would likely require bringing people in on weekends and even on third shift. As a result, even your normal price wouldn't hold. However, there might be a way to help each other.

Suppose the customer's true usage pattern was such that some units could be shipped early, others could meet the normal 60-day objective, and others could be deferred for 90 days. Here is a suggested "adjustment" that you both probably could live with. You would suggest that such a compromise might even allow you to hold to your standard price, even though you'd be accommodating the customer's need for faster delivery. You're changing a stand-off into offsetting wins.

Some buyers only feel comfortable when they know that you know they have all the marbles. *They can say no or just fail to act.* However, if you have made good progress with an Account Development effort, they may not have this power position any longer. Part of the strategy of Account Development is to take this leverage away from them. The leverage changes hands when you achieve executive support for your problem-solving proposals. During this process, you manage to take away or otherwise neutralize their right of last refusal. When this happens, they will know it, but you can't let them think that you know it. You will merely play out the process as if you never imagined that leverage, and who has it, was a part of the process.

NEGOTIATION

Usually, if a negotiation is going to take place, a specific subject has surfaced as more important to one party than to the other. By inference, one or both parties believe that the other has room to maneuver, and further, (to make a transaction more fair) that the other should give something up. If either party is operating under constraints that cannot be subject to negotiation, but the other party is not aware of these constraints, or refuses to believe that they are real, then there is the probability that a stalemate will occur and the transaction will not materialize.

In the world of selling, it seems that customers want to define negotiation as something that the seller must give away in order to get the business. They will use every leverage possible to achieve this one-way negotiation. A frequent leverage ploy is to suggest that a competitor would gladly meet the terms under discussion and therefore, you should also. Usually, if you fold with this customer, you will also be compelled to fold under the same pressure in all subsequent transactions. Rather than remaining a negotiation, it has become a concession—and one that the customer pressured you into. The customer has won and believes that you lost. The perception is that the customer "found you out" and got what he or she should have gotten all along. The customer held firm, and you conceded.

The propensity to want to negotiate, and the degree of emphasis placed upon it, is directly inverse to where you are currently operating within the ranks of the customer's organization. If you are calling at the upper management levels, you will see little or no desire to negotiate. The reasons for this are sorted out by the content of the previous chapters; however, let's highlight several points.

The executives are buying into ideas, possibilities, and potential benefits, which is what you would be selling at these levels. At this time, there are questions and the need for more information as they attempt to fully understand if this is something that they should promote and, if so, to what degree. At this level of consideration, there really isn't anything to negotiate. They know that many details remain, but that is always true with their projects, and they know that they have bright subordinates who will deal with the details later.

If your "sell" is successful at the executive plateau, by definition it has to be passed downward within the organization to reach levels where implementation can begin. As the process proceeds, more details become known and many require specific and non-revocable answers. It is within this downward spiral that negotiation as an implementation tool will surface. At some level, the customer's need or desire to negotiate becomes inevitable.

ACCOMMODATION

In our minds this is something that you do throughout the sales cycle to serve the best interest of your customer and your company. It is also something that you do to avoid future customer attempts at one-way negotiations and/or compromise. The act of accommodation may be where the salesperson has the greatest opportunity to be a real problem solver. In many situations, the salesperson does have options and alternative approaches that could enhance the overall transaction. Even so, accommodations should never be automatic or given without recognition and/or reward. We think that most sales cycles have places where an accommodation can make a real difference, particularly when it adds to the solution and apparent benefits that are going to materialize for the customer.

Accommodations don't have to be given away. For example, your product and its application might provide quicker and more dependable results if you were able to modify your usual training or provide it on the customer's site. A shrewd salesperson might carefully orchestrate training into an item on the critical path, and one that can produce the expected benefits. This salesperson is building an issue to which he or she is already holding a solution in reserve.

After having carefully manufactured unique training requirements (because of this customer's special situation), the salesperson might then strategically "admit" that training appears to be a weak link in the implementation of the project. Working with the customer, the salesperson laboriously defines all the dimensions of special training needs . . . not offering a succinct solution, but saying that he or she cannot, at this point, tell what such training is likely to cost even if it could be provided. In this situation a wonderful opportunity for an accommodation has been carefully constructed. The salesperson is about to "bend over backward" to help solve the customer's problem.

The accommodation, recognized and appreciated, is also a barrier and a defense against someone's efforts to negotiate something later. When selling, invent the opportunity to accommodate; you want to have chits to play in the latter part of the process. You should carefully let others know that you have these chits. This technique causes reluctance, perhaps even embarrassment, to ask anything more of you.

COMPROMISE

When this point is reached, both parties generally concede that each needs to move a little. It's a give-and-take situation, but each needs to do both. In most all selling/buying situations, there is some room for gentle compromising. It's better to compromise somewhere than to negotiate anywhere. Customers seem to discern the clear difference between the two. This distinction may occur because they are used to facing the need to compromise in their social/personal lives, but those environments rarely deteriorate into the act of negotiating. Negotiating seems to fit better in the business world where both parties are playing with someone else's money. It is therefore impersonal and could be thought of as just playing the good game.

HOW TO PLAY THE GAME

If you have some flexibility concerning negotiating, accommodating, and compromising, never let it be known, and never, never, do any of the three without getting something back. Otherwise, you're just a patsy and may also be perceived as always trying to get more than your fair share. If a customer begins to feel this way, it is only a short step to the conclusion that you may not be entirely honest and that they must always put you to the test, if only to get you to where you were supposed to be in the first place. If you did cave in, tell the customer that they took advantage of you and your company and that doing business this way again would not be prudent. Tell them that you made a mistake. Raise some flack. If you are forever passive, then they continue to feel they had to drive you to the fair deal and that you can't really be trusted. The upshot of this is that eventually they'll feel more comfortable doing business with someone else.

If you have very little room to negotiate or compromise, figure out appropriate ways to convey this from the very beginning. Never let it become a point of focus or an issue. Never let it become a consideration in the customer's mind. The technique for handling this is much the same as for preempting the toughest selling situations. You've got to plan for them and set up the avoidance process early on. Since we know that the further down you are on the corporate ladder, the more likelihood of encountering the problems associated with negotiation and compromise, it follows that your defense mechanisms should have already been built higher on the ladder.

It should be easy to see how Account Development and calling high will play a key role in selling those things that help build your avoidance barricades. The logic is that you may have established a contact and dialogue with upper managers with whom your current contact has little or no access. It's amazing how typical this is. They know about your contact, but you are telling them things that they did not know and that they have no easy way to verify. Additionally, they are going to use some caution about doing things or creating situations that could ruin something in which someone up above is interested. Your position is that we're now here to get the job done.

If you're employed by a company that sells products and services across the country, and that has numerous salespeople and many customers, then price integrity becomes extremely important. Prices have to be the same for all customers. If this were not so, think of the countless problems you would build in the marketplace—including legal exposure. Customer buyers who should be perfectly aware of this may still insist that one or more circumstances exist in their situation that justifies an exception. What do you do?

While there isn't a pat answer, there are approaches that you can use. First, try to get the issue of unique circumstances into an "also ran" zone. Most circumstances, when viewed in a more global perspective, aren't really unique because they, or others very much like them, are happening someplace every day. If your company issued you a price book or catalog that offered different quotes dependent upon circumstances, you'd need several strong people just to help you carry it around. Even if you see the logic and the strength of the customer's argument surrounding their circumstances, don't agree to them or admit that they warrant any type of concession. Mild understanding and small expressions of empathy are as far as you should go. But if you know the customer has a valid point, what do you do now?

You can try to get the issue (circumstance) slowly downsized into something that both parties can label as a consideration or characteristic to be looked at as part of the transaction process. Part and parcel of the consideration label is to quickly identify options and alternatives that can be associated with that consideration. Perhaps there is something that you can do with the help of your local office, particularly if you're allowed to consider options and alternatives.

In this regard, you can't allow your management to be faced with a situation where the customer has assumed an inflexible position—and where there are no identified options that might be tweaked to resolve the issue(s). Salespeople who present a "one solution" problem aren't problem solvers, and they're likely not good salespeople either. Changing the status of the situation into considerations with various flavors takes some movement and giving by both parties. Finding the "can do" positions of each party will involve both accommodation and compromise—by both parties.

Most sellers have some flexibility somewhere. Even so, the careless salesperson can get boxed into a position where no one can maneuver. The selling principal to be learned here is that when you say (or even suggest) that you'll go back and see what can be done, the customer fully expects a solution. If there were only one toy soldier left standing, that is what she or he is expecting. The customer believes that you know what your company can and cannot do. Therefore if you departed with only one option, then that option, (by default) is the expected conclusion. Never place your management, your customer, or yourself in such an untenable position. If you do it often, you'll find fewer and fewer customers who want to do business with you—because you let them down. You'll also find your management more and more difficult to deal with because you don't bring them workable situations.

PRECONDITIONED BUYERS

Many buyers are preconditioned. They can mirror characteristics they have witnessed as part of the selling methods found within their own company. Naturally there are cases where their observations leave them with a tainted view of both selling as a profession and salespeople as real and good people. Perhaps they have become aware of sales managers in their own company who wheel and deal, and still the customer didn't get the best deal available. So where are their trust and confidence when they interact with you?

In many companies, the sales force is perceived as a greedy bunch of prima donnas, i.e., they dress better than others, drive newer cars, have expense accounts they take advantage of, get to travel more, stay in expensive hotels, spring for dinners and entertainment, and make more money! So, where might their trust and confidence be when they interact with you?

Another dimension of the buyer's preconditioning is what the buyer knows or perceives to be a measurement of his or her performance. The buyer has figured out what the expectations are for a competent buyer. Recognizing that some purchasing people merely process transactions as directed, there are many others who oversee and orchestrate the final phases of purchases. These latter types may belong to organizations that school and inform purchasing people in the art of their occupation, which means they are trained to deal with suppliers in such ways that they will achieve fairness and the best terms in all transactions they administer for their company. You can gain an appreciation of their mindset by thinking about how you would function if you stood in their shoes. How tough would you be? What level of preciseness and commitment would you insist upon from the selling organization? How quickly would you push away from seller-espoused benefits that didn't directly relate to your buying specifications and objectives?

The final dimension is that while the seller may feel at a disadvantage (because the buyer doesn't have to say "yes"), the buyer often concludes that he or she doesn't have a full deck to play with. The buyer is aware that the seller knows everything about the product and its application. Additionally, the seller is likely to be much more aware of available competitive products, their prices, and associated terms. Buyers have become aware that many salespeople move about and influence people in the buyer's organization— more so than the buyer can do. Therefore the buyer is likely to be unaware of understandings the seller has already attained elsewhere in the organization. The buyer can also feel that the salesperson has plenty of time to pursue this transaction, while the buyer is overworked and only needs to get this transaction completed and get on to the next one.

All of these factors blend to form the buyer's attitude or mind-set as they go about doing their job. So how does this all unfold in the buying and selling process?

Some buyers will attempt to avoid all face-to-face contact with the seller. Everything is reduced to writing. There can be pages of questions with the requirement that each be answered in writing. In this way, the buyers escape all salesmanship and any other potentially deceptive practices. This is all done in the name of fair procurement practices.

- Depending on the nature (size and complexity) of the procurement, a short list of potential suppliers may be allowed to present and/or demonstrate their capabilities. Particularly proficient buyers will also use this occasion as an entry into additional discussions on terms and conditions. It had to happen sometime, and they have little choice.

- At this point, buyers tend to feel that any concessions they didn't have to fight for have little or no value and were given at no cost to the seller. Therefore, the process should continue.

- Schooled buyers will quickly initiate two techniques. First, there is the double MSP (Maximum/Minimum Settlement Point) concept. The buyer has analyzed the criteria for a Maximum Settlement Point on the most important issues of the procurement. The buyer is trying to figure out what the seller's Minimum Settlement Point is and works at this through the negotiation sessions.

  Buyers will also use the "range finder" price technique early on. If the seller moves too easily on price or terms, the buyer will assume that there is a better deal in a lower range and will push hard to find it.

During account development, the salesperson should have obtained copies of several customized contracts as issued by the account. Careful assessment of the terms and conditions found there will help clarify the contract criteria focused on and pursued by the company's buyers. It can also be a guide to help figure out what small concessions might be given away early. If you do this, your objective is to get good value placed on your small concession. Agree to it now and thereby build a barrier against being asked for larger concessions later. Naturally, you want to keep a score card in your mind and seek some level of reciprocity as the process continues.

Certain accommodations can be given while disguised as concessions. In fact, your accommodations are mostly goodwill gestures and, while they can be packaged to have value to the buyer, it will be a low-cost giveaway on your part. During your accommodation strategy, you have very little room for more movement. It then becomes necessary for you to simultaneously communicate movement while also communicating firmness. This is best done by talking about how flexible you have been, or have tried to be. Never offer or even hint that there is a range within your terms and conditions, never use approximation language, and never explain or attempt to justify your terms and conditions.

Be proud of your prices and all of your terms and conditions. Convey this early at the first appropriate opportunity. Your company didn't put you on the street with prices, terms, and conditions that wouldn't sell. No customer is likely to know and understand the marketplace for your product as well as your own company does. You know all about the costs, demand, value, advantages, and so on. The prices and terms and conditions weren't set for you and your customer to modify, change, or otherwise negotiate. Even so, you should understand as much as you can about how your company arrived at these parameters.

INSIGHT INTO THE OTHER SIDE—COMPANIES AND BUYERS

Every company has to establish some rules or guidelines about how they will do business. All companies buy, and all companies sell. It follows that all companies have practices and/or procedures under which they buy and sell. The smaller the company, the more similarities between the practices used for both buying and selling. In a tiny company, the same person may be both buyer and seller. When buying, such a company may pay more than they should because they have no leverage. When selling, they may charge less than they should because they need the business too much. Each transaction is vulnerable to negotiation and compromise because the buyer has so much more power than the seller. It takes a strong will for small sellers to stick to their guns.

When we look at larger companies, we begin to see a separation and difference between those practices used for buying and those used for selling. As we go on up the size scale, the selling side usually takes on structure in the form of agreed-upon terms and conditions, while the buying side is shaped by the characteristics of the individual transaction. Any number of people may be authorized to buy and, lacking formalized buying practices, they are only expected to use due diligence.

When selling to these types of buyers, you are likely to have a formalized set of prices along with associated terms and conditions, while they have only the need to exercise due diligence. The careful buyer will feel the necessity to seek the best price, the best terms, and the best conditions. What the buyer does now depends on what the seller is doing. As soon as the buyer feels the transaction is fair and honest, the sale can be consummated. Therefore, the seller's job is to help the buyer arrive at the fair and honest conclusion. The seller must maintain control; otherwise, the buyer has little alternative except to resort to negotiation. In such an event, the seller has lost all advantage because it is probable that the buyer has only peripheral skills in the art of business negotiation. His or her technique is "you give; I take." Sitting firmly on this position, and depending upon how successful the buyer feels, an adversarial atmosphere can quickly surface, in which case the sale is probably lost.

When the buyer gets some of what he or she wanted, taken from you rather than given by you, there is a subsequent probability of buyer's remorse. They will wonder what was left on the table—which they could have taken if they had only tried harder. Even after they bought, they don't have that fair and honest feeling. Contemplate what it will be like the next time this same buyer and seller meet for a new transaction. As a seller, you must always be willing to walk away from a deal; but more important, you must be able to *subtly* convey this to the buyer.

Looking at larger companies again, we find that the buying function has become specialized and operates under formalized practices and procedures. In the routine buying process, the seller has to connect less with people and more with the process. In effect, negotiation and accommodation go by the board, and the seller is compelled to compromise toward the stipulated terms and conditions set forth by the buying procedures. Many sellers get caught up in this web and never escape. This is where conceptual selling never works and where the indirect virtues of your products as well as peripheral value-added attributes are seldom viewed or considered. Your goal is to go around the web, avoid competitive bidding, put the other sellers at a disadvantage, and, finally, remove the leverage that the professional buyers think they have!

The "specialty buyer" is more closely attuned to the application or "use" of what is being bought. This buyer is most often found in companies that use your product to build their product(s). This buyer can best be thought of as a working member of the manufacturing team and, as such, your performance as a supplier becomes vitally important to the buyer and to the team. The buyer will seek every assurance that what they are buying will be delivered on time and within specifications. They expect commitments promised to become commitments delivered and will tie that into the contractual relationship. If you fail, then they fail! Therefore, you should appreciate that they use multiple avenues to check performance and insure that you and your company have the capability to deliver and the track record to prove that you do it.

These specialty buyers become very familiar with the materials purchased and how they are used. Similarly, they routinely meet with engineers, planners, and so on. They interface with the MRP (material requirements planning) process and will avoid unnecessary inventories, but will require on-time deliveries. It is in this area that they will apply intense pressure on their suppliers.

Sellers can discover that these buyers can be driven to negotiate terms and conditions that can erode your margins by increasing your costs. A "just-in-time" inventory philosophy on their end means either more inventory on your end or short production runs as well as transferring certain quality control functions to the supplier(s). Even so, the professional buyer does understand that your company must remain profitable to be a reliable vendor.

The specialty buyers prefer a close and candid business relationship with their suppliers. They need advance warnings of difficulties and cannot live with surprises. Honesty ranks high on their selection criteria. One such buyer recently said, "I don't decide what to buy—but I decide who to buy it from."

The "purchasing agent" is merely an agent. The agent isn't the user of your products and services, nor is the agent the person who decided that such products and services were needed. The agent was invented when many buying processes became cumbersome and/or routine. The agent and the agent's staff accepted the burden of keeping track of things, generating and digesting paperwork, and following practices approved by others.

In many cases, added responsibilities have been assigned to the purchasing department. They may make site visits to supplier locations and arrange supplier capability meetings where technical and competency assessments are made. This clearly means that selling can and should occur at the purchasing level.

The account development objective addressed throughout this book encompasses how you can improve your ability to work and deal with buyers and purchasing departments. Your objectives, when properly executed, should help them do their jobs better while making more sales for your company. Their existence, however, assuredly does not suggest that they buffer your ability to call on users, planners, managers, and executives. They have a reputable function. So do you.

MATT'S SOLUTION

In business-to-business selling, both the buyers and the sellers come to the table with their own (separate and different) set of terms and conditions. There are many factors that have influenced how each company needs and wants to do business. For the most part, both the buyer and the seller have legitimate business reasons and logic that support their desire to do business a certain way. Both have learned that items can be grouped into either a non-negotiable or a negotiable category. The seller must remember that few things are truly etched in concrete.

Most buyers and sellers, while making a transaction, understand the parameters and ranges in which *they* have decision-making authority. They also are aware of certain areas where some give-and-take is likely to be possible, but is beyond their authority. Finally, they know about those areas where their company cannot or will not bend. Even this final area must occasionally be put to the test, recognizing that, under certain circumstances, nothing is forever. Within this framework, it cannot be forgotten that the buyer wants to buy and that the seller wants to sell!

Matt should understand that it is unusual for him and his customers to immediately arrive at a consensus where his product meets all of their needs and where the desired terms and conditions are mirror images of each other. Part of Matt's new approach must embrace the idea that he and his customers aren't going to argue, but rather they are going to discuss issues and sort through alternatives until each finds a new and acceptable position. The salesperson has the responsibility for keeping these discussions on a congenial business level.

Matt must accept the reality that he cannot sell successfully unless his product does represent a solution to his customer's needs. Matt needs to be a problem solver. *To sell is to customize two situations until they meld into one.* The problem-solver approach will also transmit interest, innovation, and flexibility to the buyer. These are appeals that tend to cause the buyer to respond in kind.

Numerous constraints exist merely because of procedural habits. This is as true for Matt's company as it is for the customer. Therefore, there are occasions where he must sell back into his own company. To do so, he must have full knowledge of why his customer is sticking to a particular position and seems to be *unable* to move.

Finally, Matt must get out in front of the power curve with his key customer contacts. He should perform those activities attributable to the account development process as described throughout this book. While doing this, he will lay a foundation about his company and their products along with building an appreciation of his available terms and conditions. He must incorporate the elements of negotiation, accommodation, and compromise.

CHAPTER 11

ACCOUNT SERVICE INVESTMENT PROGRAM

A Tough Selling Situation:
When There Isn't Enough of You to Go Around

There will never be enough of you to go around, and this will contribute to a loss of business now and again. This is a frustrating fact of your life that can last as long as you continue in the sales profession. The trick is to change the odds so that any lost customers are not as important to you as those you are able to keep. The odds are changed by your own territory strategy and planning. While this tough selling situation will never disappear, there are ways to overcome its downside impact. Chief among these is to design and implement a customized Service Investment Program.

_____

KAREN

Four months ago Karen had completed her training and was assigned a sales territory that included 28 customer accounts, 11 named prospect accounts, and a two-state geographic area. Since then, she had made personal calls on all 28 customers and on 6 of the prospect accounts. She also added 8 more companies to her prospect list, but had not found time to do any work with this group.

Much of Karen's sales revenue depended on customer reorders. She routinely received a weekly Order Status report showing monthly order amount by customer, plus the previous week's orders and a year-to-date accumulation. She noticed three customers who were highlighted with an asterisk, indicating that their order pattern had changed—they had not ordered for two consecutive months.

Karen visited each of those accounts shortly after she took over this territory, but there had been no time for callbacks. She had already exceeded her travel expense budget, and she needed to get back on her plan. She knew that she could not squeeze any more time out of a day and that she couldn't be two places at once. On the other hand, she couldn't accept the possibility of a continuing trend where customer orders slowed and then disappeared. She was determined to sort through this and find a logical and workable solution.

_____

THE INVESTMENT ENVIRONMENT

One of the exciting features of "owning" a sales territory is that you can think of it as your own business. A sales representative can enjoy entrepreneurial feelings while avoiding many expenses that accrue to small business owners. Independent sales representatives usually do own their business, but a company employed salesperson can experience most of the same "ownership" sensations. A sales territory is something to take pride in and is the environment in which a person can achieve personal growth and business stature. It is an asset to be cherished and cared for.

In business-to-business selling, most salespeople have an assigned territory. This territory may have a geographic orientation in which all present and prospective customers within specific boundaries *belong* to a named representative. Another frequently used approach is to blend in an industry specialization ingredient so that the representative can develop greater business knowledge within the boundaries of a specific named industry. For example, a salesperson might be assigned responsibility for all credit union customers and prospects although they are located in geographic territories assigned to others. Frequently, the assigned territory will also include specific companies, which may be customers or prospective customers. In any event, the territory is usually well-defined. Large companies with diverse product lines may have more than one sales representative calling on the same customer. This may be necessary, depending on the complexity or special purpose product, but can also lead to confusion within the customer's environment.

Most sales territories have a history that dates back beyond the current representative. Unfortunately, such history is seldom an advantage to the present salesperson. If the past representative was great, then the customers may resent the departure and even assume that the new representative cannot compare. If the previous representative did a poor job, then it is likely that bad opinions were formed and were transferred to the selling company and to its product(s). This is a problem that must be faced and dealt with quickly. A new representative will not be given a honeymoon period and must quickly show a take-charge approach.

CUSTOMIZING YOUR SERVICE INVESTMENT PROGRAM

If you never make calls on your customers and have no alternative way of providing support to them, then you cannot expect to have a continuing business relationship with them. The Service Investment Program is a comprehensive plan for effectively distributing your available time. Its implementation has to be customized depending on product and buying characteristics, territory profiles, company direction, sales goals, and numerous other territory parameters. Every salesperson operates within an environment that pushes and pulls the service investment process until it shapes itself into an optimized modus operandi.

Dollars and Cents As Your Compass Heading

The charter to represent your company in an assigned territory is serious business. Whether the territory is new to you or if you've had it for some time, you need to meticulously profile its business characteristics. (Hopefully, you will have a personal computer and the necessary software to set up such a profile in an easy-to-maintain fashion.)

Your territory profile should include the financial side of your business relationship with each account. Since it's your business, you'll want to forecast revenue potential based on what has happened in the past, tempered by your best assessment of what can happen in the future. That future will depend largely on building your own *time-optimizing formula*. You'll need such a numerical compass to chart a course designed to optimize your work activities.

Most salespeople will work under a sales incentive compensation plan. Such a plan will spell out the kinds of results the company is willing to pay for. Many plans motivate more in one direction and less in others. All sales revenue dollars may not be of equal value when commissions are calculated. The incentive compensation plan is intended to be a driving force in terms of directing your sales activities.

The incentive plan coupled with your account profiles can become the basis for organizing your total territory strategy. Where you are going to spend your time is the baseline for territory planning. Since we know that your revenue projections will not be equal for all accounts, we can assume that you will plan to spend more time with some accounts than with others. Even so, you should validate your intentions by visiting each account and determining whether your projections were reasonably on target.

Performance Objectives

It is likely that you will have been assigned certain objectives such as quota(s) or revenue dollars. When these are compared against your account profiles and their revenue forecasts, you will have another dimension to add to your time-optimizing formula. For example, you may calculate the probability of a 30 percent revenue shortfall. This may tell you that present customers cannot meet your objectives and that new dollars from new customers have now become a key factor in how you use your time.

Personal Objectives

Another money dimension relates to your own earning goals. You will understand the commission incentives built into your company's sales plan and realize that this is intended to have a magnetic influence on your territory activities—pulling you in one direction in contrast to another. You can now compute your commission compensation based on the plan coupled with your projections from anticipated territory revenues. If your conclusions are unacceptable, you may want to loop back to your shortfall calculations and modify some component within that formula.

ACCOUNT CLASSIFICATION

Your account service investment will depend on your assessment of those accounts that warrant the time and effort to protect your revenue position and to those accounts you believe have growth opportunities. This analysis also identifies accounts that have neither attribute and will justify very little of your service investment. For this discussion, we will use the following plateau definitions:

1. Throwaways

2. Minimum Service Accounts

3. Protect Revenue Accounts

4. Growth Opportunities

5. Quality Prospects

Throwaways

This category can be termed inactive. These accounts have bought from your company in the past, but never in large amounts and not on a frequent or predictable schedule. If possible, some brief excursion should be made to validate that they deserve this classification and that no obvious change is on the horizon.

If they are easily available through territory records (yours or a previous representative's), you may find contact names that could form the basis for a generic mailing of product information. It is important to maintain the courage necessary to virtually ignore those accounts you have classified as throwaways. Remember that you only have a finite amount of time you can devote to your territory; any time and activity that you give to throwaways must be taken from accounts in the more promising categories.

Minimum Service Accounts

These accounts are not inactive, but their order contribution is such that it would be of little consequence if you lost one or more of them. Your business analysis effort may have already found some of them teetering toward the throwaway category, and any change in their buying habits could cause them to move up or down in your account plateau categories—but they are more likely to just remain as they are. Any demands they might make on your time would warrant a reclassification. For example, if they became an accounts receivable collection problem, or presented you with a super tough selling situation, you could justify reducing them to your throwaway group.

These accounts are worthy of a mailing on any new product information pieces that might come along and, time permitting, either a quarterly visit or phone call. You need to create your description of your minimum service/coverage plan and implement it in those accounts that you have placed into the minimum service accounts category.

Protect Revenue Accounts

These accounts buy frequently and in sufficient quantity that they are of interest to you as well as to your competition. You will have already projected their revenue into your general territory forecast and may have computed the percent of contribution by each of them. Such a percent of contribution can be a revealing number that might even lead to drop some back into the minimum service level category. Those that remain will absorb much of your territory effort.

Growth Opportunities

As the name implies, this is the highest level of your account service investment plan. You will be busy protecting current revenue in an environment where you also anticipate that you can achieve good sales increases. This is where you will spend most of your face-to-face selling time plus whatever support resources may be available to you.

Quality Prospects

Although you can build only a hypothetical revenue projection based on closing new accounts, you will know that any remaining shortfall must come from this source. Therefore, the importance of prospective customers and the amount of time you plan to allocate to prospects will be influenced by the size of your shortfall calculation. Additionally, your assigned objectives, or the company incentive plan, may also become a compelling reason to pursue new accounts. In either event, closing new account business will probably require a significant part of your personal call activities.

SERVICE INVESTMENT METHODS

Communication media and techniques make up the strongest of allies for the busy salesperson. He or she can find a productive application for most such available resources, particularly when the territory is susceptible to the type of category classification described above. Communication in this regard simply means staying in touch in meaningful ways. Generally, keeping-in-touch techniques can be reduced to four categories: phone exchanges, mailings, using your support people, and your face-to-face contacts. Since every chapter of this book deals with your face-to-face contacts, we'll touch only on the other three here.

Your Phone Link

In a busy territory working environment, your telephone must become a routine extension of your account coverage plan. Voice mail will continue to expand and can be personalized if first intercepted by someone in your office who then invites the caller to be switched to your voice mail. Car phones provide the facility to be productive in an otherwise non-productive mode and can simplify staying on top of your voice mail messages. Such "inbound" business calls, and your timely response to them, are part of your Service Investment activities. Your "outbound" phone calls will have a purpose that is a more pertinent part of your Service Investment, if only because *you* planned it. Phone call productivity is increased when it is thought of as a subset of face-to-face contacts. Your Service Investment Program should incorporate the telephone as a key part of your account coverage.

Mailings

Letters, notes, announcements, and properly packaged product information can also represent you well when you aren't there. When carefully prepared, they represent your interest in the customer in a different way than you can do on the phone. Word processing capabilities allow personalized correspondence with very little effort. When written communications become a calculated part of your Service Investment Program, they also become one of your primary vehicles used to hold onto your customers when there isn't enough of you to go around.

Company Support Associates

The too-busy salesperson has to use whatever people resources may be available. This might include administrative staff, technical support people, and locally available management people. There are advantages to be gained by letting the customer know there are other people in your company who are aware of and take an interest in them and their business.

Most salespeople use the methods mentioned above. However, they are used more spontaneously than as an integral part of a territory coverage plan. Therefore, they become less powerful than they could be. When the objective is to stretch yourself beyond what you can do personally, these alternative communication tools begin to play a more aggressive or proactive role.

BENEFITS OF A SERVICE INVESTMENT PROGRAM

The *selective* use of your time and the *selective* application of your selling activities should be expected to yield specific advantages that might otherwise be left to chance. First, you must greatly increase the odds of holding onto your sales revenue from key accounts. You will show that you and your company are a quality supplier, and you will hope to achieve the status of a most-favored supplier. In short, your service investment proves that you will keep delivering what you sold and what they bought! It will become apparent that you are delivering real service after the sale and not just an illusion of service and support. In this process, you can cause specific and important benefits to accrue to you.

You will be selling before it's time for the next sale. Happy customers will talk to each other about you and your product. They will often talk about you to people in other companies who may be potential users and buyers of your products. In this regard, you can make such an account into an incredible reference account. Occasionally, you may need the ideal demonstration location to help close a new piece of business. Building such a demonstration account, where the customer is *more than willing* to make a selling environment available to you, should be one of the specific objectives of your service investment.

Accounts who recognize and benefit from your service investment also become fertile ground for you to explore new ideas related to the application of your product. They can become your practice field because you will have earned their respect. Additionally, they will share with you the new things going on within their company that could result in new uses for your product. Such customers can be a source of ideas and techniques that you can carry into your new account sales activities.

SELECTIVE APPLICATION

The appropriate level of service investment across your territory is highly dependent upon your earning objectives, account classification, and time management. The absolute requirement for selective application of your service investment has been strongly emphasized. You must feed your garden but not the weeds! When the good stuff begins to grow there—you can transplant it elsewhere.

KAREN'S SOLUTION

Karen has been making mistakes related to the overall management of her new territory. She is beginning to note a change in the buying habits of several of her assigned customers. She is running as fast as she can to make appearances at every assigned customer, but isn't able to spend enough time at any one place to really get much done.

Karen must step back and look at her territory as a business. Then, she must design a customized Service Investment Program. Having done this, she can realistically classify her assigned accounts into one of the five territory investment plateaus, then define and use the appropriate service methods for each plateau.

Karen has found herself in a tough selling situation that defies a quick or easy fix. She will recognize this and know that there will never be enough of her to go around. Acceptance of this fact coupled with a plan on how to distribute her available time and activities will overcome the negative effects of this situation.

CHAPTER 12

IMPLEMENTING CHANGE IN YOUR ACCOUNTS

A Tough Selling Situation:
Putting on a New Face with Old Customers

Your customer contacts know you and have grown used to the way you do business. You've displayed patterns, good or bad, which they've come to expect and even anticipate. Now you have decided to change the way you do business. You intend to create and operate from a business plan. Change will include a different approach, a more professional style, and even new call techniques. However, you can't start over with a new personality, and you can't exchange your old contacts for new ones. You now want to make a consequential mid-course correction

233

*that will include accelerated efforts in selected accounts,
and less coverage in others. Your customers will sense
these changes and their reaction is not predictable. Some
of them may become nonreceptive to it.*

GREG

Greg had been selling for almost three years. His family and friends
had always thought he would be a natural in any selling job. But as
it turned out, Greg had been able to show only marginal success.
He liked people and made lots of calls in all of his accounts. He was
a good talker and used this inherent characteristic to gain rapport
and to sell, sell, sell. Even so, his customers didn't often return his
enthusiasm with their own buy, buy, buy.

Greg realized that rapport could be only surface deep and didn't
necessarily imply he was respected as a businessman. He knew
that competitive salespeople were getting much of the business
that he thought he would get. Greg was ready to face any one of
several options. The two most logical ones were to either consider
another line of work or to somehow get much better at selling. He
chose the second option.

Greg managed to be exposed to some quality sales training
based on Account Development concepts. He absorbed it and has
reduced it to those methods and activities he feels can be of immediate benefit to him. He is ready to get started and he's going to
make the needed transition.

Greg now feels that while his customers seem to like him, they
have not been taking him seriously. He knows why they respond
that way. He has decided to make his sales calls goal-oriented
activities, complete with good front-end planning. He is also going
to prove that he can be a problem-solver who is willing to understand, contribute, and follow through on issues. Greg realizes the
several difficulties involved with putting on a new face with old
customers. He also knows he has no choice.

If you are already selling, you can begin to slowly incorporate the process you've been reading about—slowly, because you are running a business. Your sales territory is your business and, while you can fix and improve certain parts of it, you can't stop and start over. In short, you can't afford the luxury of going to square one. Whatever you're doing, you have to keep plugging away, because you're at least performing at some reasonable level.

Where do you start? You could decide (1) where you need to improve the most or (2) what you could do to make a big difference in the way you run your territory. If neither of these leads you to your starting point, then we suggest a universal starting point.

THE UNIVERSAL STARTING POINT—MAKE BETTER CALLS

You can go back to the discussion of the sales process in Chapter 7, read it again and decide (1) how you're going to incorporate it into your call activity and (2) when and where. How are you going to monitor yourself so that you don't just immediately slip back to the way you did it last week? Later, you might incorporate another of the kinds of activities that can lead toward Account Development; and if you're beginning to also make better calls, your investments are going to pay off faster. Making better calls is a starting place that can't fail.

The universal starting place, "make better calls," must be more than a thought on your part, and it must be more than an intention to do a better job in your face-to-face selling. Otherwise, you will tend to use your present call approach, but to just try harder.

The sales process is comprehensive. We doubt that many people can study it and then immediately incorporate it into their calls. Initially, you should use only one or two key pieces of the process. For example, do you think you could learn to listen better? If you could, you would learn more and get better at solving problems. Your customer would pick up on your attentiveness and be willing to share more with you. If you want these advantages, then just practice *using open-ended questions* and *listening*. Since you're working on only two things, you'll be able to judge how well you did.

It is reasonable to ask how your established customer contacts will receive and react to you when your calls begin to take a different shape. We think you can slip the change in without them even being aware. For example, suppose you had been making monthly calls on Fred for over two years. Today you're going to call on Fred again and consciously use and measure your success by *asking a question* and then *listening*. After the hello part, you say, "Fred, I often wondered just how you go about figuring out the order quantity each time you place an order for my products—would you explain that to me?"

If Fred is slow with his response, you must overcome *any urge* to utter another word. Fred will respond, and you should momentarily ponder what was said. If it makes sense, you can pursue the subject with a closed-end question such as: "Fred, it seems as though ordering that way does keep your inventory low; however, it doesn't take advantage of our quantity discount pricing. Would you be interested in an ordering technique that could let you have the best of both objectives?" In the past perhaps Fred thought that you seldom listened to much of what he said; but while the above conversation is in progress, Fred isn't thinking of the past but is only aware of what is happening now.

Making better calls by using the sales call process is an ideal way to get more productivity from your call time in such a way that your customer hardly notices your new approach. You might later make a note of what technique you used so that next time you can reinforce it by using that same technique plus one or two new ones. Since you're putting on a new face, give your customer an opportunity to adjust to it.

ANOTHER WORKABLE STARTING POINT—UPPER MANAGEMENT CALLS

Revisit the idea of the invisible sales cycle as described in Chapter 2. Whatever your product or service might be, think about what activities, now or in the future, might occur within the invisible cycle that could have some effect on the demand for your product . . . or other products like yours. Remember that those people who operate unseen (on the invisible part of the sales cycle) start processes that ultimately cause products and services to be purchased. Think about management people, somewhere above the users and the buyer, who could be involved in planning changes that could cause them to have even the slightest interest in a product like yours.

Ask yourself what kinds of events cause a need for your products and services.

When your customer experiences a greater demand for their products, do they need more of yours? If so, do they anticipate such an increase? Are they doing something new and unusual that they believe will generate such an increase? What is it? What are they doing? How can you discover what they are up to? If they have plans to expand their product line, how might this effect your sales to them? Suppose, however, that they were contemplating abandoning one of their product lines—could this have an impact on you?

You probably can think of several account actions that could have an effect on your sales to them. If you want an opportunity to get advance information about these things, then you must begin calling on upper management. They operate in that area that we have called the invisible sales cycle.

Even if you have a "seen everywhere" product, but your customer uses large quantities of it, then their upper management has probably thought about it . . . or should think about it. They may not think about a specific product, but they do think about expense categories. We suspect that products that do the things your product does have surfaced in conversations somewhere on the Invisible Sales Cycle. After you've figured out what might happen on the Invisible Sales Cycle, find a "call higher" target and plan on how you're going to make your move by reviewing Chapter 6 (Calling High) and Chapter 8 (The Special Sales Call). If you have some concerns, select an upper management call where you have little or nothing at stake. By definition, you probably won't have much to gain with such a call, except practice and confidence. An account with a locked-in competitor may be a good target for you.

If you're working in an account where you are well established with lower level contacts, but have never demonstrated your new "call high" notions, you could be in for a bit of trouble. Usually, these contacts will not want you to call above them and may ask (or tell) you not to do it! They *will* think, and *may* say that any business that you want to do with their company can and should be done with them or with someone at their level. Now you're really putting on a new face and *they do not like it.*

In such situations, the following three approaches have been successful:

1. It is better to ask for forgiveness than permission. You make the call and when they find out, or when it is to your advantage to tell them, you just give them your bewildered expression while exclaiming that you never had any idea that they would care or be concerned. You can follow by suggesting that you only wanted their management to know that your company appreciated their business and that your sales training classes firmly recommended occasional courtesy calls on executives. In any event, the deed is done and they'll learn to live with it. Use care to prevent them from accepting this one deviation while telling you

that you must never do it again. You cannot allow them to hold to such a position.

2. The second approach requires more imagination and work. You invent a situation or series of questions that cannot be answered or responded to by your lower level contacts. For example, you want to invite Mr. or Ms. Big to be a speaker at a group you are associated with. You want to ask Mr. or Ms. Big if his/her company would consider sponsoring *something* (anything). Perhaps your product is such that you can even build a realistic business reason for having to go upstairs. In any event, you can pre-announce to your lower level contacts what you are going to do and why. They will recognize the validity of your need and the fact that they cannot accommodate you in the matter.

3. The third approach is a shortcut and is always defensible. You are going to (or did) call on Mr. or Ms. Big because your manager (or management) has instructed you to do so. You have no choice. If you can't make it happen, then they'll do it for you! The use of one of your company executives to join you on the first such call in a specific account adds validity to this approach.

ACTIVITY-BASED STARTING POINT

While the timing will be different for each of you, there will be a day when you are ready to start a business strategy plan for your sales territory. It is remarkable how beneficial it is to view a pragmatic written document that describes the way things are as well as what things should change and how the changes might happen. This effort causes the need for specific activities to become obvious. Such a strategy is not written in a single sitting but is built piece by piece. It need not be a trying or complicated process.

One approach has only three broad sections:

• Your best descriptions of the way things are

- Your assessment of possible improvements
- Activities that could lead to the improvement

For Example:

Iron Stamp, Inc.

The Way Things Are:

1. Have three contacts at user level

2. Do about $30,000 annually

3. Have to ask for every order

4. They also buy from three other suppliers

Possible Improvements:

1. Need more info . . . such as the total expenditures for like products

2. Could introduce new Dry-fast application

3. But only to Plant Manager

4. Get bigger share (from competitors)

Activities:

1. Meet cost accounting Manager Test for volume discount applicability on bigger share

2. Use our Engineer on Plant Manager call

3. Create and present a Dry-fast proposal

4. Ask Plant Manager and staff to look at it

Your first cut is likely to be larger and more specific. The key is that it doesn't take much time or effort to quickly see possible activities that can explore new ground.

This can be done for each of your accounts as well as for your prospective accounts. As you perform the activities, there will be some accounts in which you are unable to see the improvements you hoped to achieve. In such cases, check to insure that you are providing enough account coverage to protect your current position—if that position even warrants protection. It would be understandable if you chose to reevaluate and reclassify some accounts.

GREG'S SOLUTION

Greg knows he needs to make improvements in many areas. He has congratulated himself on having the insight and courage to reflect on the reality that for three years he had been sliding through on natural instincts. He now recognizes that while these can be useful assets, their value in selling must be complemented with proven techniques applied with skill and discipline. Greg has decided that his first step will be to implement all the recommended pieces that will lead him toward making more productive sales calls. Whether or not he has vocalized the attending tough selling situation, his instincts have caused him to sense that many of his present customers will not accept a "new" Greg who acts differently. He is determined to press on in a tactful and professional fashion.

Greg has made the turn. Armed with the Account Development concept coupled with an enhanced awareness of personality types and power communications, Greg has accepted the challenge of making quantum improvements in his one-on-one sales calls. He has begun the process.

Greg experiences success and discovers that he had been more concerned about changing his modus operandi than his customers appeared to be. They could have reacted differently, but Greg carried out new call techniques cautiously and *skillfully*. Because of this, his customers began to have an appreciation for his sincerity and willingness to suggest new and better ways for the application of his products. Greg will continue to do a better job. He will move ahead and achieve the benefits of calling higher up the managerial ladder. Greg will become a consistent winner!

APPENDIX

Personality and Selling Summary
(Outlined for Busy Salespeople)

I. Profile of a Natural Salesperson

   A. Good people psychologist

   B. Successful

   C. Instinctively does the right thing, but doesn't know why

II. Personality Types

   A. Three basic types

     1. Dominant
     2. Detached
     3. Relational

   B. Everybody relates in all three ways, but most are primarily one type.

   C. "Dominant" characteristics

     1. Controlling
     2. Competitive—winning is the only goal that matters
     3. Status conscious
     4. Insensitive
     5. Tends to distrust people
     6. Independent, individualistic—"my way or the highway" attitude

7. Absolutely dominates relational types and often surround themselves with people they can easily push around
8. Frustrated by detached types; cannot stand being ignored

D. Dominant salespeople

1. Approach is competitive and high pressure
2. Generally not planners; want to be part of the action
3. Try to take control immediately
4. Assume they know what the prospect needs
5. Information well-organized but may not relate directly to prospect's needs
6. Objections are rarely analyzed
7. The close (gaining agreement) is their strength
8. Information and records seldom organized and updated
9. Follow-ups are rare and superficial
10. Dislike analyzing themselves, but dislike losing even more

E. Dominant prospects

1. Distrusting; afraid of being exploited and defeated
2. Want to deal with top people or people dominant enough to earn their respect
3. Hidden question: Are you good enough to get my business?

F. Most effective approach—smooth dominance

1. Prove you are tough and competent without defeating them
2. Plans should be thorough
3. Opening should be brisk and business like, but not threatening
4. Ask open-ended questions and listen actively

5. Information should be brief, well-organized and absolutely correct
6. Analyze their objections carefully before you answer
7. Conclusions should be direct and forceful, but not demanding
8. When the deal is made, get away as quickly as possible
9. Follow-up should be brief and businesslike

G. Detached characteristics

1. More comfortable with things, ideas, or numbers; feel uncomfortable with people
2. Do not understand emotions and try to avoid them
3. Like order and predictability
4. Independent; want to be left alone
5. Open-minded and objective
6. Relationships with other detached people are comfortable, but distant
7. Regard relational types as illogical and emotional
8. Regard dominant types as illogical, emotional bullies

H. Detached salespeople

1. Approach is logical, impersonal, and low pressure
2. Excellent planners
3. Opening statements are impersonal and lack attempts to build rapport
4. Diagnosis of objective facts is thorough
5. Present information in a factual and logical manner
6. Listen carefully, provide information; however, cannot handle stalls or hidden objections

      7. Improve on areas which they have mastered, but will not work on real weaknesses

I. Detached prospects

      1. Distrust and dislike dealmakers
      2. Hidden question: Would you manipulate me?

J. Most effective approach—impersonal logical, factual

      1. Know all the facts
      2. Opening should be brief and impersonal
      3. Ask fairly specific questions to get information you need
      4. Explanations should be detailed with extensive supporting material
      5. Understand exactly what an objection means, then answer it logically
      6. Suggest the most logical action
      7. Final proposal must be documented completely
      8. Follow-up should be thorough, and make contact only when you have something to discuss

K. Relational characteristics

      1. Need other people's acceptance and approval
      2. Happy being part of a group
      3. Good listeners and sensitive to other people
      4. Cooperative and compliant
      5. Givers
      6. Constantly ask for reassurance
      7. Insecure; easy to exploit and manipulate
      8. Relate well to other relational people
      9. Allow dominant people to bully and exploit them
    10. Detached people really frustrate them

L. Relational salespeople

      1. Approach is to make people like them

2. Focus on the person, not the business opportunity
3. Openings are warm, friendly and much too long
4. Acquire a lot of information, but much is irrelevant
5. Communications are vague and over-long
6. Listen carefully, and sympathetic concern makes it easy for prospects to raise hidden objections
7. Closing is their greatest weakness
8. Spend too much time chatting after the agreement
9. Follow-ups are generally excellent
10. Cooperate with training efforts, but resist working on real weaknesses

M. Relational prospects

1. Easiest ones to call
2. Hidden question: Do you sincerely care about me?

N. Most effective approach

1. Friendly dominance
2. Plans do not have to be detailed
3. Learn something about their personal interests
4. Communications should be warm, friendly, and unhurried
5. Direct conversation toward areas you must explore, but accept occasional detours
6. Information should be brief; not impersonal, but expressing warmth in a businesslike manner
7. Closes should be forceful, but friendly
8. Chat for a few minutes when your business is complete
9. Follow-up is most important

III. Allow Your Personality to Work for You

    A. Primarily dominant

        1. Soften your general approach
        2. Spend more time on planning and diagnosis
        3. Listen carefully; look for hidden problems and confusion
        4. Concentrate on dominant and relational people

    B. Primarily detached

        1. Show caring for other's interest and problems
        2. Openings should be longer and friendlier; information shorter and harder-hitting
        3. Probe for hidden concerns
        4. Ask repeatedly for agreement and carefully check your progress
        5. Stay involved with products and services that require analysis and concentrate on detached people

    C. Primarily relational

        1. Try to be more forceful and analytic
        2. Don't worry about whether people like you; trying too hard for acceptance actually costs you respect and new business
        3. Plan more carefully
        4. Make openings shorter and more businesslike
        5. Check your status repeatedly

IV. Conclusion

    A. We all have primary personalities

    B. Assess yourself as well as others with whom you communicate and do business

C. Your opinions will have more impact when you have made an effort to understand the other's personality

The Sales Process
(Outlined for Busy Salespeople)

Insight: Assume you aren't doing it as well as you're capable
of doing it, and perhaps not even as well as you
once did it!

I. Planning

   A. Objective

       1. Qualify new prospect
       2. Learn more about qualified prospect's prob-
           lems and resources
       3. Make a sale
       4. Reopen lines of communication with inactive
           customers
       5. Follow up on a sale
       6. Provide a service

   B. Results of last contact

       1. Recorded information helps reopen your rela-
           tionships
       2. Prospect will be impressed by your under-
           standing of his or her needs

   C. Type of person

       1. Describe, using adjectives

           a. dominant, detached, relational
           b. young or old
           c. cautious or impulsive
           d. trusting or suspicious
           e. friendly or unfriendly

   D. Make certain you have all necessary pre-call infor-
       mation

II. Opening

    A. Sale before the sale

    B. Objectives

        1. Identify yourself and your company

            a. Speak slowly
            b. Pronounce your name clearly and say a word or two about your company

        2. Make rapport-building statement

            a. Refer to anything the prospect can be proud of
            b. Refer to a mutual friend
            c. Refer to something in common
            d. Communicate understanding

III. Diagnosing

    A. Benefits

        1. Present right product or service
        2. Make most convincing sales points—link directly to prospect's needs and problems
        3. Create mutual problem-solving atmosphere
        4. Increase prospect's receptivity by listening and trying to understand
        5. Make more sales calls

    B. Information-gathering techniques

        1. Get the prospect to talk
        2. Make gentle attempts to change the subject
        3. Ask open-ended questions
        4. Actively listen

            a. Concentrate
            b. Shut up
            c. Never interrupt
            d. Use silence

      e.   Keep your mind open
      f.   Show that you understand

C.   Integrating the techniques (advantages and disadvantages)

   1.   Active listening

      a.   Provides maximum amount of information
      b.   Much of information may be irrelevant

   2.   Open-ended questions

      a.   Provide more control than active listening
      b.   Obtain more information than closed-ended questions
      c.   Can be time-consuming
      d.   Some information will be irrelevant

   3.   Closed-ended questions

      a.   Give maximum degree of control
      b.   Provide exactly the information you need
      c.   Do not provide important information that you do not request
      d.   May irritate prospects

   4.   Use all three techniques, switching from one to the other as necessary

D.   Conclusions

   1.   Intentions are more important than techniques
   2.   Critical question: What is the prospect's problem?
   3.   Prospect's ideas determine reaction to your proposal

IV. Presenting

A.   Set clear objectives

    B.   Organize your presentation

        1.   Opening—Overview of discussion
        2.   Body—Detailed information about each major topic
        3.   Summary—Restatement of major benefits
        4.   Close—The pay-off

    C.   Keep it short

    D.   Emphasize benefits, not features

    E.   Encourage dialogue

        1.   Understand prospect's problem
        2.   Emphasize benefits that apply
        3.   Adjust to prospect's reactions as you encounter them

V.   Closing—Ask for something!

VI.   Overcoming Objections

    A.   Clarification

        1.   Basic technique: Restate objection as a question, then pause for reaction
        2.   Valuable effects

            a.   Gently forces prospect to indicate whether your understanding is correct
            b.   Shows that you take objection seriously
            c.   Prospect will become less defensive, more willing to be open
            d.   Communicate respect and desire to understand without reinforcing objections by agreeing with them

    B.   Classification of objections

        1.   Stall

            a.   Any reason give to postpone action

               b.   Some are legitimate; some are rationalizations

         2.   Hidden (characterized by)

               a.   Illogical objections
               b.   Large number of objections
               c.   Refusals to accept good answers to objections

         3.   Easy—Based on misunderstanding or lack of information
         4.   Hard—Desire for benefit that your product does not offer

     C.   Answers to objections

         1.   Stall—Stress value of prompt action and danger of procrastination
         2.   Hidden—Probe for underlying objections
         3.   Easy—Provide necessary information
         4.   Hard—Minimize missing benefit; stress benefits offered

     D.   Restate benefits and close

         1.   Test to make sure prospect accepts answers to objections
         2.   Restate benefits
         3.   Move your call ahead

VII.   Following Up

     A.   To the customer you are the company

         1.   Take opportunity to stand out
         2.   Customers will be more satisfied with your products
         3.   More likely to buy again and recommend you to their friends

Presentations
(Summarized for Busy Salespeople)

Insight: Scan this before every presentation. Let your eyes
rest for a few seconds on each item and think
about how it may apply to your presentation.
Please make a call planner first. You can be sure
that these few minutes will make a difference.

I. Pre-presentation logistics

   A. If at your place

      1. Sign up for the meeting room
      2. Enlist your helpers
      3. Check that everyone knows the way

   B. If at the customer's place

      1. Visit the room now
      2. Get the customer to assign a helper
      3. Check availability and condition of equipment
      4. Gather info on their meeting customs

II. Presentation day

   A. Arrive early for set-up

   B. Greet meeting members as they arrive

III. Take charge from the beginning

   A. Stand up and explain the purpose and agenda

   B. Find your friendly faces

   C. Focus on your decision-makers

   D. But relate to everyone

IV. Get into the swing of it

    A. Forget about you

    B. Relate your message to them

    C. Make the audience participate

V. Remember to exercise your delivery techniques

VI. Think about how you organized your content

    A. You're ready with a solid opening

        1. Does it lay out your expectations?
        2. Insure that they agree to this

    B. How many key points are included in the body?

        1. Don't forget the presentation aids
        2. Remember to validate and link

    C. Your summary must be inclusive—Stress benefits, benefits, benefits

    D. Give them a strong close—Ask for your objectives

VII. Depend on the basic selling skills

    A. Read Appendix B again

    B. Picture yourself doing these things:

        1. Keeping your points short and crisp
        2. Selling and selling, not telling
        3. Sharing a good story/analogy
        4. Making your visual aids work for you
        5. Showing them your enthusiasm

    C. Watch for and react to their feedback

        1. Show sensitivity
        2. Solve problems together
        3. They don't owe you anything

4.   So earn what you want

VIII.   Conclude on a high note—You must have agreement
on the next step

INDEX

259